What Clients Have To Say

As a CEO and senior executive of smaller to Fortune 100 publicly traded firms, I've had the pleasure of being involved in at least a hundred executive searches over the last thirty years. Lyn is simply the most thorough executive recruiter that I've worked with. His business process orientation combined with a keen ability to listen and advise in a value-added manner allows him to synthesize recruitment needs into actionable and results-oriented steps that optimize a client's return on effort. His business acumen combined with leading executive search capabilities set him apart from the rest of the crowd. That's why I will continue to call upon Lyn for my executive search needs.

President/CEO, Utility-Based Holding Company (AMEX)

Edwards Executive Search, by far, offers the most economical, thorough and comprehensive process to identify top executive talent that I have encountered in over 15 years. More importantly, Lyn consistently delivers results in placing superior candidates. He really is in a class by himself in recruiting high-level executive talent.

SVP/COO, International Construction Company (AMEX)

We have worked with Edwards Executive Search for several years now and find Lyn to be extremely dedicated and thorough in finding the right individual for us. He is an excellent evaluator of executive talent and character, and understands the needs of our company. His practice utilizes innovative techniques to help give us a thorough picture of each candidate, and he does so in an economical and concise manner. I do not hesitate to refer him to others in need of a successful, cost-effective executive search firm.

SVP/HR, Energy Holding Company (NYSE)

Your process is superior.

Managing Director, Big 4 Accounting Firm

It's All About the Fit!®

"We're from Edwards Executive Search Mr. Burton,
and to be honest we are after your scalp."

It's All About the Fit!®

A Practical Guide to Hiring an Executive Who Will Increase Your Company's Value

LYNTON EDWARDS

New Insights Press

Editorial Direction and Editing: Rick Benzel Creative Services
Cover and Book Design: Susan Shankin & Associates
Cover Illustration: Kyle Platts
Title Page Cartoon: Peter Dodsworth
Chapter Opening Page Cartoons: John Morris page xii;
Aaron Bacall page xxii; Roy Deldado pages 14, 54, 100;
Fran page 28, Tim Cordell page 36; John Morris pages 46, 66;
Bart page 88; Andrew Toos page 114; Mike Shapiro page 124;
Jessica Hagy page 132; Ralph Hagen page 140

Published by New Insights Press, Los Angeles, CA

First edition printed in the United States of America

Library of Congress Control Number: 2018931272

ISBN: 978-0-9984850-6-5

To my client companies and candidates

Contents

"Hello, sir. I'm Charles Henderson and
I'm head of a successful executive search company."

I EARNED MY MBA from a very good business school. I am proud of that and of the school. One semester I decided to take an HR course. I went to speak to the professor who was chairman of the human resources department. His office was deep in the basement of one of the buildings, tucked away in some dark corner. Perhaps the professors were assigned offices based on seniority or a lottery system, but I can tell you that the finance and accounting professors, who were the "rock stars," did not have offices in the basement.

Given the location of my professor's office, the experience of where I found him was an eye-opener for me. It was the beginning of my awareness and thought process about the oft-downplayed importance of human capital in the success of a business.

In today's complex and highly competitive business world, hiring the best human capital is critical to a company. We used to call them "high performers," but in my view, that term is too vague and does not sufficiently describe the type of executives that a competitive, ambitious company needs to succeed today. That is why I prefer to call them "Value-Builders," a term much more indicative of what an executive in a key position is supposed to accomplish. A Value-Builder is what you want for any C-level position.

Value-Builders are people who deliver accomplishments that positively, meaningfully, and consistently add to your company's bottom line. Research indicates that the quality of an organization's executive team makes a meaningful difference in a company's valuation. The results of a survey conducted by Deloitte and reported in *Deloitte Insights* states that a company with effective senior management receives as much as a 35% valuation premium, as the quality of a senior leadership team ranks 2nd as the most important criteria that investment analysts use to judge company success.

The Deloitte survey of 445 investment analysts goes on to say that the effect on valuation of having superior senior leadership is greater on smaller companies than on larger companies. Thus it is especially essential to hire Value-Builders if you are a small- or mid-sized enterprise (SME). Such companies today exist in a highly competitive marketplace, challenged from both the top and the bottom. SMEs have to run fast enough to outpace the many smaller upstart and hungry companies below them, while seeking to catch up to or not be squashed by the giants above. Survival depends on consistently growing and increasing your revenues, not just maintaining them. Your future depends on improving the profit contribution of incremental revenues, or by increasing margins to become more profitable if revenues happen to be stagnant. This means that your executive team cannot afford to miss revenue growth opportunities or bottom-line improvements, or fail to continually drive operational enhancements. They have to be able to function consistently and resiliently at the highest levels to build value.

Presenting a More Effective Methodology for Hiring a Value-Builder

The common thinking among business executives is that hiring a key C-level executive can be based largely on examining a candidate's past work experience and using it as a predictor of future performance. If a person has been successful at Company A, demonstrating top performance qualities, the thinking is that you can be fairly confident that he or she will bring the same strong results to a new job at Company B.

Believe me, this is myopic thinking. You cannot simply look at past experience as a predictor of someone's ability to perform well enough to drive up value in a different situation. A person may have produced strong results in Company A, but when you move them into the same or similar position (or an even higher position) in Company B, it's a different story. No two organizations or situations are the same. Every company, every job, every challenge, and every team is different. So many factors can affect performance and effectiveness. The competencies you acquire in a newly hired executive may simply not bring on the same results when he or she steps into your position.

Relying on past experience as an accurate predictor of future executive performance is like picking stocks based on past performance—a flawed strategy. Past achievements are never a guarantee of future success. As a *Harvard Business Review* article by Sabina Nawaz says, studies show that there is a 50% chance that a new executive will leave the hiring organization within the first 18 months. The reasons stated for this alarming statistic include poor cultural fit, inadequate onboarding, or the lack of appropriate expectations.

This book will teach you a better way to find and hire the right Value-Builder for any specific position. The methodology needed to do this must be robust, thorough, and sophisticated. There are multiple steps or elements to getting this done. My methodology is precisely the full court press you need.

The heart and soul of my executive recruiting methodology is called the CompleteFIT® executive search process because it uses a variety of tools to ensure that a candidate matches a company's needs in every key dimension. The CompleteFIT process helps you look at four areas of alignment for each candidate to verify whether the person is truly the exact Value-Builder you need *in that specific executive role*. The four areas include Technical/Experience-Based Fit (of course), Personal Fit, Cultural Fit, and Ethical Fit—and combined, they act as a sort of four-legged stool.

The CompleteFIT executive search process is structured, disciplined, rigorous, and holistic. There are several important elements to it. Chief among them is that my process uses proven scientific, state-of-the-art assessment tools to evaluate a candidate's competencies, motivation, and personality-based behavior. These allow you to determine whether the person can truly take on the responsibilities of the position and achieve your desired goals. What's unique about these tools is that they help you accurately understand how someone thinks and behaves not only in good times, but also in stressful times, when issues and challenges often cause people to change how they think, process information, treat others, and problem-solve.

A corollary critical part of my process is that I emphasize that you must specifically pre-determine the type and degree of both hard and soft competencies that are needed for value-building success in the position you are seeking to fill. You must pre-think the standards you need the candidate to meet to provide a context, if you will, so you are not simply judging people in a vacuum.

In this book, I will teach you how to conduct your own CompleteFIT process for hiring Value-Builders. Whether you are a CEO searching for an executive for your team, or an HR leader involved in hiring your firm's highest-level executives, my goal is to help you learn how to improve your ability to find, hire, and quick-start truly great Value-Builders for your company.

About Me

I am not an academic. I am not an industrial psychologist. I am a professional headhunter, a practitioner of high-level executive recruitment. As such, I am interested in practical solutions, not theoretical ones.

My background has prepared me for this role. I am the former CEO of a privately-owned company, a corporate executive of a large multi-national company, and a former member of the Board of Directors of several companies. I have learned firsthand the criticality of having a top-performing, effective management team.

As my career indicates, I write with experience of what I will impart to you in this book. I have practiced these principles. I understand what it takes to lead a company as the CEO/President and I have been personally responsible for increasing a company's profitability and valuation. Early in my CEO career, I learned that if I didn't have the right people in the right positions, MY own success would be affected. I have witnessed firsthand the practical benefits of having a top-performing management team of Value-Builders—and I admit, I have also felt the pain of making mistakes in hiring.

For the past decade, I have been a C-level retained executive recruiter, aka, a headhunter. As a "retained" recruiter, I am hired upfront by client companies to find, assess, and place the right person into a specific high-level job they seek to fill. Most of my clients are seeking C-level executives, including CEOs, COOs, CFOs, VPs of operations, sales, marketing, or finance, and other top-level management positions. As such, I must constantly strive to provide my clients with the most professional, current, and relevant business advice, as my livelihood depends directly on how effective I am in finding the right candidate for each position.

In my executive recruiting practice, I give my clients a two-year replacement guarantee. This is longer than most retained recruiters offer. But, if the CompleteFIT process works, it should be longer, don't you agree? In my view, if a key executive is not in a company for at least two years, their impact cannot be very significant. A tenure less than that is not enough time to develop and implement strategies and actions, see results, and tweak the strategic and tactical initiatives to further improve results. I therefore need to "get it right" the first time. I believe that I have been doing the job well, as I have successfully placed hundreds of executives with close to a perfect record.

Hiring a Value-Builder will help you increase the value of your company. In fact, it is one of the most important factors, if not the most important, that is in your sphere of influence. Investing effectively in human capital is no different than investing in other types of business capital, say capital equipment, for instance. A professional, robust, rigorous, and sophisticated process of recruiting and hiring will increase the chances of making the optimal hire and ensuring you get a good return on your investment. Having an effective process is the key to resolve any complicated business issue or challenge — and that fully applies to recruitment and hiring. I am a process person, having earned an MBA, a Master Career Coach designation, a Black Belt in Lean/Six Sigma, and a Black Belt in Tae Kwon Do — all highly process-driven activities. And I have applied the power of process to my executive recruitment practice.

Let me add that I am convinced that this process must also evaluate candidates from a *holistic* perspective. For a smart, talented executive to be a top performer and Value-Builder for you, for that person to thrive and deliver meaningful results, the holistic nature and alignment of the fit between the company, the position, and the candidate must be strong!

The scientific assessment tools that I discuss in this book were not developed by me, and I take no credit for them. I simply use them, along with other techniques that I will discuss, to get done what I need to get done. I do believe, however, that the combination of tools, techniques, and methods that I use in my executive search practice is unique. My methodology, as a whole, is designed to accomplish my definition of what a good headhunter does — i.e., find and place Value-Builders — and in this book, I offer my advice to you.

If you are reading this book as a CEO or C-level executive, or the VP of HR of a small- to mid-sized corporation, I am confident you will take away valuable new insights on how to go about your own hiring process based on the CompleteFIT methodology and recommendations you will learn here. I wrote this book to help you improve your own approach to search for, identify, assess, and hire Value-Builders so you will be empowered with the same knowledge and acumen that I bring to my clients resulting in successful recruitment and hiring.

LYNTON EDWARDS

a.bacall

"I'm a headhunter and I try to match highly skilled candidates with corporate clients. A degree in sociology of marsupials simply won't qualify."

Chapter 1

Why a Value-Builder?

I RECENTLY HAD A client firm that was growing at a rapid pace by acquiring and integrating competitors. Rolling up the industry, they call it—buy and integrate, buy and integrate. The CEO was spending a lot of his time managing each integration because he correctly believed that if the integration of the companies did not go well, he should not have made the acquisition in the first place. But, he realized, because of the time he was spending on the integrations, important longer-term strategic issues for the company as a whole were not being thought through and developed. So he decided to hire a VP to handle strategy development.

He found some candidates from the industry and began interviewing them. He had used all the right recruiting "tricks"—multiple interviews, group interviews, interviews over dinner, reference checks, and so on. Eventually, he found Jim Wolf (a pseudonym in this book). Jim was one of the smartest guys the CEO had ever met. He was thrilled and hired him.

Unfortunately, Jim knew he was smart and began acting like it. He treated others as if they were dumb and only he had the right answers. Nobody in the company liked him or wanted to work with him. Jim had not shown this type of behavior throughout the interview process. Of course, nothing in his resume had indicated he had such "issues." And his references apparently didn't want to say anything negative that might hurt him!

So, despite the time-consuming search that had been undertaken, the CEO let him go. The failed hiring cost the company big-time, not only in out-of-pocket costs, but in disruption and delay in dealing with the vital strategic issues that the CEO wanted resolved.

Investing in Human Capital

The story of Jim drives home an important point: human capital, more than ever, is a key driver of profitability, innovation, and sustainability. In my view, the primary goal of an executive team is to increase the value of their business unit. Other financial measurements—EBITDA, Gross Margin, various ROIs, and so on—all factor into valuation. But they really only matter if the value of the business enterprise increases.

There is solid evidence to support that your hiring the right key executives absolutely makes a difference in this regard. As I pointed out before, the Deloitte survey of 445 financial analysts who are in the business of determining a company's valuation concluded the following:

- The senior management team's effectiveness ranked as the 2nd most important criteria in determining a company's financial success.

- A company with an effective senior leadership team received a higher valuation from the analysts, as much as 35% higher.

- The effect of the senior leadership team on valuation was greater on smaller companies than larger ones!

If the quality of your leadership team is so critical, when you have a key management opening, shouldn't you utilize an executive search process to ensure that you are bringing in the right candidates and then selecting the optimal one who will perform at the level you need and expect?

Many large companies hire an industrial psychologist to help them assess candidates, but that is very pricey. Smaller companies are hard pressed to afford those types of resources. According to Compile®, and this is not news to anyone, there are a lot more small- and mid-size companies than larger ones that need to worry (even more so as reported by *Deloitte Insights*) about hiring the best executives:

- Revenues of < $50MM = 5,682,000 companies

- Revenues of $50MM to $500MM = 38,700 companies

- Revenues of $500MM to $1B = 2,400 companies

- Revenues of $1B+ = 2,900 companies

Today, even a company with revenues of $500MM is not all that large.

These smaller companies must get their hiring just as right as the larger multi-national companies with millions of dollars in recruiting and candidate assessment resources.

What is a Value-Builder?

Based on my experience as a CEO and senior executive as well as an executive recruiter, small- and mid-size companies must focus on hiring "Value-Builders" in their key executive positions. Let me make the following distinctions to help you understand what a Value-Builder is. I read one article that defined three levels of performance among executives:

- A HIGH PERFORMER. These are executives who exhibit a high degree of performance, consistently being proactive in addressing challenges. As "A" players, they deliver results and do it without casualties. They seek solutions and encourage others to solve problems.

- A NEUTRAL PERFORMER. These executives are not detrimental, but they are not high performing either. More like "B" players, they do add some value, but not as much as you really want or need. They mostly maintain the business and they do that well. But they do not meaningfully improve the enterprise.

- **A DETRIMENTAL PERFORMER.** These executives may work hard, be loyal, appear effective, but they really don't help make progress at all in terms of improving the effectiveness and efficiency of their particular function. They are "C" or even "D" players, who ultimately get in the way of progress.

Of course, no one really wants to hire a neutral B player or a detrimental C or D performer (and if you have any F players, shame on you!). In my view, companies should do better than hiring even A-list players. That is why I add this fourth type of executive to the hierarchy:

- **A VALUE-BUILDER.** These executives are among the elite of top-performing "A" players. They drive meaningful economic improvement. They possess an impressive blend of skills that have a constant and consistent positive impact on your company's performance. These executives have a clear sense of the company's purpose and their specific role in delivering successful results at every turn. They generate actions on their own and lead others with deep insight and exceptional skills of analysis, reason, and persuasion. They have the ability to take advantage of new opportunities that surface, and they can also effectively handle the challenge when there are problems or obstacles to surmount. They are intensely cognizant of the bottom-line implications of their decisions, so they operate with a clear view of the economics of every situation and the financial benefits at stake. When something happens that adds to the bottom line of the firm, it can usually be traced to the work of a Value-Builder.

In short, a Value-Builder has what it takes, that little bit extra, the combination of competencies that deliver results time and time again. Do you know what I mean? You've heard it before: they operate as if they were the company's owner, not driven just by sales growth or gross margins alone, but on total value creation.

In today's business world, it no longer suffices to hire just high performers if their efforts do not actually result in increasing the value of the firm. What is critical to your company is ensuring that, from this day forward, any position you hire is filled by someone who can accomplish a range of critical tasks that accordingly create value, such as the following:

- Providing outstanding leadership that inspires engagement of everyone in the organization

- Developing strategic plans and initiatives that take the company to new heights

- Implementing innovations and creating new ideas that ameliorate the company

- Increasing the productivity of those who report to them

- Cutting costs and bringing new efficiencies to your company

- Anticipating issues and problems and getting a head start on their resolution

These are the Value-Building leaders you need. Their actions result in economic improvement that brings on higher valuations among investment and financial analysts, as well as in the financial markets and lending institutions.

You Need a Robust, Thorough, and Sophisticated Hiring Approach

How do you identify Value-Builders? How can you distinguish them from "just" the A players? Based on my experience as both an executive and an executive recruiter, I can tell you the answer—it requires a meaningfully more robust approach to recruiting, interviewing, assessing, and hiring. You cannot find and hire Value-Builders using the traditional techniques of just collecting resumes, eyeballing past achievements and experience, checking references, and interviewing. That approach may find "A" players, but will it not help you hire true Value-Builders whose fit into your company must be far more precise and effective, allowing them to thrive and deliver consistent Value-Building results while utilizing all of their talents.

The most common mistake companies make in hiring into key executive positions is making the assumption that the accomplishments listed on the resume of any candidate are a dependable indication of the future results you can expect. As I have stated, the achievements an executive has accomplished in the past do not ensure their effectiveness in *your position, within your team, in your company culture.* Each situation is unique, and may call for different or a different degree of skills, competencies, attitudes, working styles, and values.

Many CEOs and HR people believe that hiring is an art, with a human side to it, and that they have "a nose" for assessing the right person to be a key player in their company. They believe they can look at a resume, interview the person, and judge how his or her past experiences will align with the goals they have for the position they are hiring.

I concur that recruiting has an artful side, but it is not enough to find and hire the Value-Builder you need in that specific job. It takes a far more sophisticated and scientific approach to identify a true Value-Builder. The candidate assessment process you need to use must involve measuring people's "hard" and "soft" behavioral competencies, attitudes, values, and motivations—and then matching those competencies to the specific requirements of the specific job they will take on. I am talking about a serious line-by-line comparison, not just an overview. The devil is in the details. This means that you must take the time to effectively identify in advance the specific and detailed personal and cultural attributes and competencies the job requires so you know exactly what you are looking for in a candidate.

Examples of a Bad Fit

When the skills, competencies, and values of the candidate do not align with a particular job, it can lead to major disappointment and wasted time and money. Consider these stories.

SITUATION #1

John Tower, CEO of Standard Manufacturing, was coming up on his 12-month mark in his new role and it was painfully apparent to everyone that he was not delivering on the great expectations the Board had placed on him. They couldn't understand how someone with a career of progressive successes, beginning as a bright up-and-coming MBA and culminating with a successful five-year run as CEO of Kendrick Industries, could be failing so miserably at Standard, a company that on the surface seemed very similar to Kendrick.

John's story is not that uncommon. His reduced effectiveness was not because of any technical incompetence he had or lack of experience. He just wasn't a very good fit to the position of president of Standard. The dynamics and challenges that Standard faced as opportunities or roadblocks were not the same as those Kendrick had faced. The market circumstances, company inclinations, and resources were different.

Michael Watkins in his book, *The First 90 Days*, surveyed senior HR practitioners who agreed that the challenge for an executive coming in from the outside was "much harder" than when promoted from within.

Standard's Board made a hiring mistake. Their hiring process was inadequate. John was not an effective leader for the position at Standard despite his accomplishments at Kendrick. His strengths did not align with what the company needed to increase its economic value. In fact, his particular weaknesses were damaging in that role. It was their own fault, and the business suffered. It didn't have to be this way!

SITUATION #2

Susan Smith was a hard-driving executive who worked her way up the ladder through several successful consumer product companies. She had been very effective working at the executive level in a mid-sized company ($200MM) when it was acquired by a much larger strategic buyer. She was among several execs who lost their job due to the consolidation. She swore to herself that she wouldn't go through that again. So she took a job as COO of a smaller ($75MM) family-owned business. The president of the company (a member of the family) told her that they were interested in growing the company at a steady but sustainable rate; and they had no interest in being acquired by another firm. She sighed with relief.

Unfortunately, however, within three months, she grew impatient with both the cautious approach and the "lack of business acumen" of the president. She couldn't hide her impatience with him. Staff, loyal to the president, began to complain about her attitude. She went from being a high performer at her previous employer to an average, detrimental performer at her current employer.

The problem was that she lacked sufficient self-awareness to recognize that she was not cut out for life in the "slower" lane of a smaller company. More importantly, her new employer didn't bother to effectively assess her motivational profile and how it aligned with the company, a step that could have and should have been done! She was clearly competent to do the job, but she just didn't fit in the new role! So, she failed.

So, What About "OK" Performers?

There are many stories about bad matches where the fit is so wrong that the executive does not stay very long, gets fired, or quits in frustration. These hiring mistakes are costly.

Obviously, hires this bad should be avoided.

But I would also suggest that the hiring of average performers or OK performers is not to your benefit and should also be avoided.

An article in *Scientific American* said that top performers produce 20 to 30 times more than the average employee in their field. And, in a *Harvard Business Review* article, "The Challenge of the Average Employee," Anthony Tjan writes:

> "They (average employees) can be a drag on those who are the best. While not everyone can be above average, the more mediocre talent you have in a business,

the more likely it is to have a negative effect on those
who can really make a difference. This creates reten-
tion and motivation issues for your highest performers. There will always be a distribution, even if it is
a forced curve, of talent potential and capability in
a business. But the goal should be to raise the overall average of the entire pool, and avoid letting it get
pulled down."

Of course, every company will have some average employees; but that doesn't mean that you shouldn't aim higher.
That's what I will be teaching you to do.

Executive
Search
Inc.

"I DO like people . . . but not a WHOLE LOT."

Chapter 2

The Four Elements
of a CompleteFIT®

VOIDING A BAD or mediocre hire is why I have committed myself to executive recruiting based on what I call having a CompleteFIT between the job and candidate. Far more than any other recruiting methodologies that I am aware of, the CompleteFIT process evaluates candidates in multi-dimensional ways, at a deep level, to assess:

- Their track record of performance and results delivered in an accurate, metric-based format

- Their intrapersonal and interpersonal competencies

- Their behavioral tendencies that can be either strengths or barriers to career success

- How they react under pressure or stress

- The motives, values, and drivers of their work ethic and performance delivery

- Their cultural attitudes that indicate how well they will fit into your organization, and

- The relevancy and transferability of their experience, and success in increasing your company's value

My method involves, in addition to an evaluation of each candidate's experience-based, technical skills, an extensive evaluation of the person's personal and cultural skills based on scientifically-validated psychological and intellectual assessment tools, backed up with specialized interview techniques I have found to be very effective in understanding the candidate accurately and completely.

CompleteFIT Executive Search

The comprehensive nature of my methodology is based on the premise that there is more to an alignment between the individual and the job than the usual primary focus on someone's experience in the field. In my process, a CompleteFIT is actually comprised of four dimensions of a candidate that must be evaluated. Let me walk you through these dimensions at a high level for now.

Technical (Experience-Based) Fit

 This element of CompleteFIT refers to a candidate's business background and track record. Obviously, this is the type, scope, and nature of their past experience and its relevancy to your company. The experience-based Technical Fit is the most common starting point in recruiting, though it is mistakenly often the only element that companies look at in detail, and therefore effectively. Of course, it is a critical element that must be evaluated in assessing candidates and gaining assurance that they actually have the work-based professional experience, skills, and competencies to do the job you want. It is clearly the most basic level of fit.

All good recruiters try to evaluate a candidate's experience-based competencies effectively. Of course, the key question is just how effective their techniques are in that regard. In my view, you need to go beyond the simple listing in a resume of past work experiences and/or stated accomplishments to examine it deeply and understand precisely what the candidate's experience involved.

Personal (Position/Job) Fit

 For an executive to perform at a very high level, of course they need to have the specific and unique technical, experience-based skills we just discussed. But what about the non-technical skills, those that impact their ability to communicate, to motivate others, to form relationships, to lead others, to be resilient, to persuade, to anticipate, to offer ideas and solutions? I could go on and on. These "soft skills" are just as crucial for business success as the more recognized and easily understood "hard skills."

People are not automatons. Each individual is unique, with a varied set of personality and behavioral characteristics that come to work with them each day and significantly affect what they do and how they do it.

Personality drives behavior. If innovation is part of your personality, you will behave innovatively. If it isn't, you probably won't. Organizations need to examine the dimensions of personality that each candidate will bring to the job and assess whether their combination of behavioral strengths will drive economic improvement or conversely will be a weakness (and we all have them) and get in the way.

Another element of Personal Fit is a candidate's critical thinking style and cognitive ability and style, which can make a big difference in achieving results. Some executives tend to take an in-depth, deeply thoughtful approach to evaluating information and making decisions. They keep digging for facts, which may delay the decision-making process. Others like to make quicker decisions, perhaps based on gut feelings and experience-based intuition. Some executives are great at dealing with big picture issues, while others are better at focusing on practical solutions to a clearly identified immediate problem. They may be more disciplined in their thinking. Some are better than others at detecting errors, gaps, flawed information, projections, assumptions, etc.

There is no right or wrong here. What you want is the cognitive style that matches what you need for top performance in that specific job.

Cultural (Organizational) Fit

 The third element of a CompleteFIT is Cultural Fit. I define culture as the "motivational infrastructure" of your company. Each organization, both consciously and unconsciously, creates an environment that people at every level can sense and feel. Culture permeates throughout a company, from how to talk to others, to whether the leadership team tolerates diversity of opinion and disagreement over direction and strategy, to how decisions are made, and more. People will either thrive, just get along, or stumble because of their reaction to the culture.

Every organization values certain skills, talents, and competencies. Executives who have these qualities are noticed, get promoted, and perhaps receive larger bonuses. If there is strong alignment between the motivational infrastructure of your company and the motivational profile of an executive, the culture will automatically motivate the executive.

Ethical (Business Values) Fit

 The fourth element of The CompleteFIT refers to alignment of the candidate's ethical or business values with the company's—and yours. In my view, ethics can be a real "tie breaker" in deciding whether to hire someone. If you believe a candidate is not in strong alignment with the business values and ethics of your company, *caveat emptor*, buyer beware.

In his book *Why Smart Executives Fail*, Sidney Finkelstein wrote the following passage that I completely buy into:

> Perhaps the single most important indicator of potential executive failure is one that is hardest to precisely define . . . the question of character . . . a person who has high ethical standards and deep competence, who desires to succeed by helping others to be better than they would otherwise be on their own, who can face reality even when it is unpleasant and acknowledge when something is wrong and who engenders trust and promotes honesty in the organization that they create and lead.

Can there be any doubt that a candidate who has the right skills needed and aligns as specifically as possible in all four of these elements would be more effective for you than some-one who does not?

How Scientific Assessment Tools
Help Assess a CompleteFIT

To ensure the tightest CompleteFIT possible, I employ a set of proven personality and cognitive assessment tools. These are a significantly better way to assess the "soft" elements of CompleteFit. While not infallible, they offer detailed and insightful information that can be used to predict more accu-rately a candidate's potential professional performance in a specific position. Of course, there are other pieces to an effec-tive hiring puzzle. But I am convinced that adding some objec-tivity to a largely subjective process is a smart thing to do.

There are many varieties of scientific assessment tools from which you can learn much about your candidates. The tools I have been utilizing in my executive search practice are the Hogan® battery of assessments. I have been using these tests for more than a decade and find that they are highly effective in providing useable information about a candidate that helps both my client and me gain a clearer sense of the person's behavior, working style, motivations, and values. When used as I suggest, these assessments can be surprisingly predictive of professional performance.

The very smart people at Hogan break the skills needed for strong business performance down into four skill sets, each with a list of characteristics as shown below.

BUSINESS SKILLS

- Demonstrates keen insight and application of budgeting, financial practices
- Identifies short-term objectives and steps to achieve them
- Demonstrates an understanding of industry knowledge and trends
- Gathers, organizes, and analyzes diverse sources of information
- Generates creative ideas and perspectives
- Recognizes and works within the political environment of the company
- Effectively presents ideas and information to others
- Detects errors, gaps, and potential flaws in goals and tasks
- Identifies solutions given available information
- Effectively demonstrates, promotes, and sells products and services
- Effectively expresses him- or herself through written communication

LEADERSHIP SKILLS

- Assembles cohesive groups based upon required skills, goals, tasks

- Demonstrates keen insight and application of business policies and procedures

- Uses sound judgment to make timely and effective decisions

- Assigns work based on task and skill requirements

- Provides support, coaching, training, and direction to peers and subordinates

- Effectively implements new methods and systems

- Manages disagreements between individuals or groups

- Monitors performance, providing feedback for improvement as needed

- Fosters energy for and provides direction towards organizational goals

- Coordinates people and materials to maximize productivity and efficiency

- Develops strategies to accomplish long-term goals

- Recruits, rewards, and retains individuals with critical skills and abilities

INTERPERSONAL SKILLS

- Listens and restates ideas and opinions of others for mutual understanding

- Develops collaborative relationships to facilitate goals
- Goes beyond job requirements to help the organization
- Persuades others to a desired result
- Explores alternatives to reach outcomes acceptable to all parties
- Expresses himself/herself effectively through verbal communication
- Demonstrates loyalty and dedication to the organization
- Creates customer loyalty through courteous, timely, and helpful service
- Enjoys and seeks out interactions with others
- Collaborates with others to achieve goals
- Respects, values, and leverages individual differences

INTRAPERSONAL SKILLS

- Driven to accomplish goals and complete tasks
- Deals comfortably with unclear situations and problems
- Driven to exceed the performance of others
- Displays sensitivity towards the attitudes, feelings, and circumstances of others
- Performs work in a consistent and timely manner

- Performs work with care, accuracy, and attention to detail

- Willing to receive and accept new ideas, approaches, and strategies

- Adheres to direction, policies, and/or legal guidelines

- Pursues goals despite obstacles and/or challenges

- Coordinates and directs routine activities effectively

- Acts in accordance with job-related values, principles, and standards

- Accepts personal accountability for actions regardless of outcomes

- Takes appropriate chances to achieve goals, considering negative consequences

- Believes in oneself to accomplish tasks and goals

- Actively acquires knowledge, skills, and abilities to remain current with job requirements

- Handles pressure without getting upset, moody, or anxious

- Plans work to maximize efficiency

- Acts with honesty and integrity

- Displays a positive disposition towards work

- Exhibits hard work and diligence

I find that to be a very impressive list that speaks to the combination of skills necessary for strong business performance. Assessment tools like the Hogan battery of tests help you get at these four domains of skill sets, yielding valuable insights into the professional and personal qualities of your candidates relative to how their personal skills, competencies, motivations, and values align with the position you need to fill.

In his *Harvard Business Review* article "For Senior Leaders, Fit Matters More than Skill," Jean Martin reports that Ingersoll Rand shifted its approach to assessing potential leaders, focusing not just on qualifications but on four "fit categories" — knowledge, values, career experience and leader behaviors — which in combination produced a more complete view of an executive's style and how he or she is likely to approach work. I find the Hogan and Ingersoll Rand's models to be very similar in their message.

In my experience, assessments tools help paint an informative "holistic" picture of a person that allows you to go far beyond what you derive from a resume or from a subjective, intuitive judgment based on an interview. Someone who is outstanding in these business, leadership, interpersonal, and intrapersonal skills is far more likely to be a Value-Builder; and I have never known a CEO who doesn't need or want more Value-Builders on his or her team.

In addition, when the results of these assessment tools are combined with your own analysis and judgmental evaluation of a candidate, you can arrive at a much clearer decision regarding whether you have found not just any Value-Builder, but the one who has the tightest alignment with your job. That is how I gain the confidence needed to know I have a CompleteFIT—when there is a strong, very tight alignment between the candidate and position.

There are many assessment tools available other than the Hogan assessments I use. However, please note that while some of these assessments are good, some are not. So be careful when selecting which of these assessment tools you use.

I started using Hogan because the company requires that one must be certified to use them. To me, this meant that the tests are robust and sophisticated enough to require training. As the Hogan people state, effectively using such tools involves more than just giving the tests. You have to be able to read the results and scores, and then to draw useful, multi-measurement conclusions. If you don't know how to intelligently use them, how helpful can they be? I am certified and re-certified in the Hogan assessments and they have worked well for me.

To hire the elite of top performers, the Value-Builders, it takes a process this powerful to be able to evaluate the multidimensional qualities and competencies of a candidate, and then to assess to what degree those qualities and competencies are in alignment to what you need to increase the value of your business enterprise.

"Do you think this would work for the Wilkin's account?"

Chapter 3

The Importance of Fit

B EFORE WE EXAMINE how you can implement the CompleteFIT process in your hiring, I want to discuss briefly why it matters that you seek to have the tightest multi-dimensional fit between your position and any executive you hire.

If you Google "How to Increase Your Company's Value" you will get more advice than you could possibly read. If you look closely, there is a common thread in all of the advice — it is not easy or simple to increase your company's value. Why?

Valuation measures the health and power of your company at any given time by persons or entities who have or may be considering a financial interest in your firm. In today's world, business and commerce have become extremely complex.

There is serious competition in every industry. Your profitability, and thus your market value, depends on the ability of every executive on your team to make good decisions, consistently.

The skills and competencies needed for strong performance and effectiveness are specific, detailed and most certainly to some degree unique to each executive position in your organization. This means that to have an effective team, you must match each leader's personal strengths to the competencies needed for success in their job. There must be a very high degree of alignment not only in terms of the nature of each executive's work experience, but also in the degree of the skills, thinking ability, behavior, and character of the executive to meet the challenges that his or her job calls for.

When the alignment is off, it is not an optimal fit, or even worse, it is a bad fit. The impact of an ineffective executive is degressive, rather than accretive. Every executive on your team must be accretive in my view. Today, companies that hire and retain high-level executives who do not align well with their job are at risk of being very disappointed, because the ramifications of a less than optimal or bad fit are multiple.

First, there are domino-effect consequences on employees when you do not have a CompleteFIT. Let's say that your company is growing and expanding rapidly. A less-than-optimal hire could trigger a loss of strategic continuity or a possible management disruption, with employees becoming confused about the direction and priorities of the company or about their responsibilities. An arrogant, insensitive, or micromanaging executive, who is otherwise smart and experienced, can cause employees to lose their own motivation to apply themselves or even to choose to leave the company entirely rather than work for someone who does not value their efforts and contributions.

Does this matter? Yes, of course it does; we know it does. A study from Development Dimensions International Studies showed that engaged employees are 21% more productive and 60% less likely to seek other employment than those less or not engaged. This suggests that ensuring you hire an executive who will forge this engagement is absolutely to your benefit.

Secondly, customers can be impacted by a bad or mediocre hire. They might defect to competitors because they don't like a new executive's policies, pricing decisions, return practices, lack of emphasis on customer service, approachability, etc.

The Real Challenge Today

As far as I know, no one intentionally hires a less-than-optimal executive. Yet the incidences of poor choices and bad fits are shockingly high, and the impact is serious. Consider these statistics cited in various publications from a wide range of consulting and research organizations:

- Nearly 80% of job turnover is due to hiring mistakes (Harvard/DBM)

- 40% of new managers fail within the first eighteen months of a new position, usually for non-technical reasons (The Hay Group)

- 80% of executives do not have the people skills for effective leadership (Human Capital Institute)

- Two-thirds of managers fail as they are unable to build and maintain functioning teams (Hogan, et al.)

- The average failure rate of recruited executives in their first year is between 40% to 50% (a 2001 study of executive failures conducted by the Executive Search Information Exchange)

I mean, what is going on? How hard can it be?

Overview of an Effective Methodology

Your challenge is to get ahead of the possibility of failure by hiring Value-Builders right from the start. You need to approach talent acquisition in the same analytical way that you evaluate other ROI-oriented investments. This requires a methodical process, with steps that help ensure you identify, recruit, assess, and then hire the right person for each position.

Here, in a nutshell, is an overview of the methodology that I follow to ensure a CompleteFIT.

Edwards Executive Search Methodology
PRE-SEARCH ACTIVITIES

- Detailed Position Specification Prepared
- Technical (Experience-Based) Competencies Determined
  - "Must Have" Competencies vs. Preferred Competencies

- Personal (Job) Competency Standards Determined
- Cultural (Organizational) Competency Standards Determined
- Business Values Scenarios Determined

  Result: Complete detailed set of search standards established

SMART CANDIDATE SOURCING

- Concentric Circles of Searching by Industry Relevance Determined
- Technology-Based Outreach to Find Passive Candidates
- Job Postings to Find Reactive Candidates/Applicants

  Result: A reasonable number of potential candidates identified for further evaluation

TECHNICAL EVALUATION AND SELECTION OF LEADING CANDIDATES

- Initial Resume Review to Identify Candidates of Interest
- Request, Obtain, and Review Candidates' Self-Evaluation (Experience Matrix)
- Request 3-year salary history

  Result: Identify list of candidates to interview

INTERVIEW SELECTED CANDIDATES

- Contribution-Centric Based Interviewing
- Behavioral Interviewing

  Result: Candidates selected to complete the assessments

TOP CANDIDATES ASSESSMENT

- Leading Candidates Undergo Assessment Tests (Using Hogan® Assessments or other scientific assessment tools)
- Based on Assessment Results, Candidate Alignment with Standards Analyzed
  - Personal Fit Standards
  - Cultural Fit Standards

Result: Finalist candidates who demonstrate tightest fit with standards selected

COMPLETEFIT® FINALIST CANDIDATE(S) SELECTED

- Additional Information from Finalist Candidate(s) Requested
  - Business Values Credo & Scenarios
  - Candidate Statement of Truth
  - Written Explanation of Career Job Changes
  - Consent to Conduct Executive Background Check
  - Consent to Confirm Educational Credentials
  - Names of References (360°)
  - Relocation Acknowledgment (if applicable)

Result: Absolute finalist candidates rise to the top of the list

COMPLETEFIT® FINALIST CANDIDATE(S) PRESENTED TO CLIENT

- CompleteFIT Candidates Selected
- **Process Repeats Itself Until Position Filled**

Result: A true Value-Builder has been found who is a CompleteFIT with the company

POST-HIRING ACTIVITIES

- Onboarding Support Using Emotional Intelligence-Based 1-on-1 Mentoring
- Scientifically Determined Candidate Management Insights to Client

  Result: A high performing, and highly satisfied executive assimilates into the company and produces superior value-building results

In the rest of this book, I will walk you through this methodology, including the CompleteFIT executive search process, which I consider the most important part of the overall methodology.

Let's start with the Candidate Sourcing activities.

"Hi, guess who just got head hunted."

Chapter 4

Setting Up Search Standards and Smart Candidate Sourcing

O BVIOUSLY, BEFORE YOU begin assessing and selecting candidates, you have to find some good ones to consider.

However, what most companies fail to do when they begin searching for candidates is to carefully spell out in adequate detail what they are looking for. While they may write a job description, it is seldom precise enough when it comes to identifying the very specific skills and competencies needed. Nor does it sometimes take into account at a meaningful depth the specific type of experience and background that would best support the role the candidate is expected to play.

This is why the CompleteFIT process puts great emphasis on pre-setting specific standards that you want candidates to match before you even start the search process. Without these detailed specific standards, you risk relying entirely too much on subjective judgments about a candidate's background and abilities to accomplish the goals and objectives you have in mind for the position.

Determining the Depth of Experience You Need

In my process, the first key element in identifying potential candidates is to decide on the extent of direct industry experience you want. Do you need someone whose background is primarily or even exclusively in your specific industry, so you know that the person has real experience in what you do? Or are you willing to broaden your search to include candidates coming from related industries, or even outside of those related industries? And, if so, just how do you define the nature of a "related" industry? One with similar products or services? The same customer base? The same selling channels, etc.?

I use an approach that I call the Concentric Circles of Industry Relevancy to determine how close or far away from the direct, competitive industry I should search for candidates. I distinguish between four levels of industry relevancy in terms of how extensive I make my pursuit of candidates:

- *Primary industry relevancy* — candidates who have worked for direct competitors

- *Secondary industry relevancy* — candidates who have worked for companies with similar products or services, are selling to similar types of customers, through similar channels, etc.

- *Tertiary industry relevancy* — candidates who have worked for companies that sell tangential or somewhat related products or services

- *No industry relevancy* — candidates who come from outside these three levels and have no experience whatsoever in what the company does

Example of Concentric Circles of Industry Relevancy for a CFO Search for an Energy Measurement Company

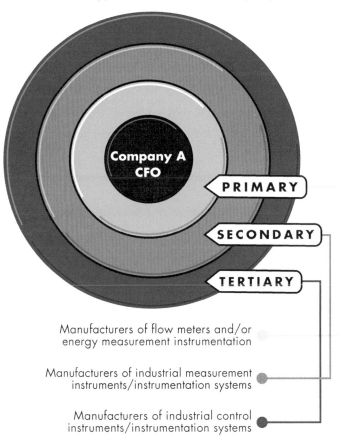

PRIMARY

SECONDARY

TERTIARY

Manufacturers of flow meters and/or energy measurement instrumentation

Manufacturers of industrial measurement instruments/instrumentation systems

Manufacturers of industrial control instruments/instrumentation systems

You can set up your own concentric circles to define your potential spheres of interest as broadly or narrowly as you want to guide your candidate-sourcing activities. You can search in a very focused manner, or go broader to consider a variety of candidates from other industries related, to your desired degree, to the products and/or services you offer.

Two Types of Candidate Sourcing

As for how to find candidates, there are two types of sourcing you should do. You cannot rely on just one or the other to get the job done in a thorough manner. I define these as:

- *Proactive sourcing.* You identify happily employed candidates (called PASSIVE candidates) using outreach technology, such as LinkedIn® Recruiter. This is the tool that I use and find to be most effective. It allows you to identify potential candidates who are not looking for a new position. Some ambitious executives, however content with where they are, are always interested in considering a challenging new position. If they agree to listen and learn more, they may become even more interested and willing to consider a move. Of course, that is why I am called a "headhunter."

    Let's say that you are seeking to hire a CFO for your plastic injection molding company. This technology allows you to search a database of professional people using keywords. LinkedIn's database, for example, includes millions of profiles. Put in the title, the industry or industries, the name of any competitors or channel partners, education level if relevant, location if that is important, and so on. And voilà, with the push of a finger, all matching profiles are identified that you then can contact via an InMail. And so a dialogue begins.

I get about a 60% response rate from such unsolicited contacts, which my LinkedIn account executive says is as high as she is aware of. Many hiring executives tend to favor these passive candidates because they have a bias against candidates who are "in transition," i.e., out of a job. They may wonder, *"Why did the consolidation affect her . . . why didn't they keep him . . . was there a problem of some sort . . . if she is so good why didn't they find another position for her?"* In fact, 90% of my placements are passive candidates and only 10% are candidates who were in transition.

- *Reactive sourcing.* This refers to good old-fashioned job postings on platforms such as LinkedIn, CareerBuilder, Indeed, and so on. Of course, these job-seeking websites service candidates who are mostly in transition without a current job for one reason or another, or unhappy or restless for some reason in their current employment.

In today's world there are in-transition candidates who are outstanding and should not be eliminated from consideration just because they are looking for a new position. I use the major "job boards" and have also had good results by identifying and using smaller "specialty job" positing sites. For a CFO, for example, I have used FENG, the Association of CPA's, and other industry associations that allow for job postings. It may take some digging to find these niche job posting sites, but they are out there and deliver candidates that the major job boards seem to miss.

Suffice it to say that for an optimal search, you need to do both proactive and reactive candidate sourcing! In the old days, many professional recruiters would brag about their candidate "database" or candidate sourcing "network" as the reason to hire them to conduct the search. In effect, they were pitching that only they had the edge in identifying candidates. Today, LinkedIn Recruiter, and other similar technologies *are* the database. If you use this type of technology in the right way, no one else has a better database or network at their disposal.

Promoting Internal vs. Hiring External Candidates

As long as we are talking about how to search for candidates, this is a good time to address the issue of hiring from within versus going outside the company. Given the importance of having Value-Builders and the risks and consequences of hiring the wrong person or average performer, you might wonder if you shouldn't just promote from within, reducing the risk of bringing in an external candidate who could turn out to be a square peg in a round hole. Here's my advice on this issue.

First, there are times when promoting someone from within to a higher-level executive position makes sense. A qualified internal employee knows the company, its culture, policies, and the people on the executive team. So the risks of having a poor alignment or a complete hiring failure should be reduced. Promoting an individual from within is also well received by other employees who are themselves encouraged to see hard work and contribution rewarded. So all things being equal, an internal promotion is preferred.

But be a little careful. An internal candidate may not always be the right Value-Builder you need. The internal candidate may be a good performer, but not an outstanding one. As noted earlier, each job and its context must be considered unique. An internal candidate's prior experience and track record cannot be assumed to be a guarantee of future success in a new role, especially if that role is broader or more demanding.

The fact is, a company can often benefit from recruiting outsiders who can bring in a fresh perspective or different skill set and personal strengths that can prove valuable in navigating a new strategy or implementing new operating procedures. I've worked with companies that needed a transfusion of new blood to revive a tired-out culture stuck in its ways, or to refresh a stagnant business model, offer new insights, or new energy.

The decision to promote from within or recruit externally can go either way—it's up to you to decide if you have the right candidate internally or if searching outside makes sense.

If you are debating a decision to promote from within or recruit externally, my advice is to conduct an executive search process so you can compare any well-chosen internal candidate(s) up against some highly-qualified external candidates of interest using the CompleteFIT process discussed in this book. An apple-to-apple comparison will help you determine which candidate is the true Value-Builder and the best choice for you. I just don't believe that you should settle for second-best for a key management position.

"That mover you headhunted for me turned out to be a shaker."

Chapter 5

Setting Your Value-Builder Technical Fit Requirements

A S AN ELEMENT of your pre-search activities, I cannot emphasize enough that you must do a detailed self-assessment of the qualities, skills, personality styles, and ethical values that you are seeking for the position. Recruiting a Value-Builder cannot be conducted in a tunnel vision manner, focusing only on what the candidate can offer you without a specific and detailed understanding of what you need, and a thorough comparison of the candidate to those criteria.

In this chapter, I will focus on my process of helping clients determine the technical, experience-based requirements.

Writing a Position Specification (Not a Job Description)

Many companies believe they can understand a candidate's technical competencies simply by writing a generic job description and then comparing each candidate's background to a rather general list of requirements during the interviews. Determining the experience-based fit cannot be just some subjective assessment based on examining a candidate's resume, eyeballing their career history, and surmising the depth of skills and experience the individual may have.

That is the lazy way out. I have found that such a document usually misses the mark when it comes to identifying in full detail the skills and competencies you are looking for and their relative importance. A job description is usually too general, and there is also a tendency to fall into "HR speak," using standardized language and euphemisms. Even if you have numerous follow-up interviews with candidates, you may draw inaccurate conclusions about whether the individual has the skills and background that align with what your position needs. Not to mention that most executives are really not very effective at interviewing.

Must-Haves vs. Preferred Skills and Competencies

This is why I work with clients to convert a job description into a "Position Specification" document. In this document, the company starts with a very detailed self-assessment of the technical experience and capabilities they are looking for in a candidate. This requires creating a list of the specific work background, skills, and competencies needed for the position. Moreover, these must identify *line item by line item* what relative strength is needed for each. The more specific the criteria you can list in each area of technical assessment, the better you will be able to make a solid judgment about a candidate. This list becomes a robust benchmark against which you can assess each candidate.

In creating this document, I recommend that you write down 5 to 10 absolute "must have" experiences and competencies. One of the advantages of this concise list of "must-haves" is that you can eliminate most candidates quickly when you begin receiving resumes. It'll be easy to decide whether they have these competencies, or they don't!

Next, you supplement this list of experience-based "must-haves" with a list of additional "preferred" experience-based competencies that can contribute to ensuring you hire a Value-Builder. What other experience-based skills do you want the prospective hire to have demonstrated in their prior career? Describe them with precision in a list. Be as detailed as possible.

This process of self-assessing and pre-defining your required and preferred experience-based skills serves as a highly effective first step in the recruiting and interviewing process. As you can see, this process is far more detailed than simply writing a job description and interviewing candidates, subjectively assessing the level of their skills and competencies vis-à-vis a list of general criteria.

Remember, the "must-haves" can have no exceptions, in general. I stick to this rule 99% of the time. But to be honest, on occasion, I can be fascinated by an interesting resume of someone who appears to be a great "business athlete," a candidate who has had impressive accomplishments in a variety of companies, industries, and positions, an ambidextrous executive, if you will. So there are times when I want to know more. A lot of recruiters may not have the guts to stray too far from the written job criteria, but I believe you may occasionally uncover a superstar this way.

You can find an example of a Position Specification in Appendix A.

The Experience Matrix

Once I have completed the initial resume screenings and have a number of candidates who look interesting on paper (this usually is about 10% of the resumes reviewed), I do something that I believe is unusual: I ask those selected candidates to fill out what I call an Experience Matrix, which is a listing of each of the desired experience-based Technical Fit competencies that you developed in advance of the search process. The list includes the degrees of industry relevance, the "must-haves," and the preferred competencies.

The goal of the Experience Matrix is to allow you to truly assess what I consider the key metrics in any recruitment:

- What exactly were the business results the candidate claims to have delivered and how much credit is due to them for those results? It is useless to put any reliance on the person's prior title, how many people reported to them, the size of the business unit, the size of their office, or what floor it's on! Rather, you need to know what precisely were *their* accomplishments?

- What role did the candidate actually play in achieving any stated accomplishments? Was he or she the prime mover, a meaningful contributor, or just an active participant? Not that being an active participant is a bad thing, but you need to understand the truth behind the nature and extent of their contribution as you consider the candidate for your position.

- Exactly what happened metrically to their area of economic responsibility during their management of it? Every position has some sort of economic responsibility, a role in improving the profitability of the enterprise. How did they really do?

- Look beyond the stated accomplishments. Are the skills that drove the individual's contribution to strong results transferable to your company? Given the role(s) they played, have they already successfully done what you need done and can they do it again in your company?

All candidates of preliminary interest receive this Experience Matrix, and I then ask them to score themselves in terms of the degree or level of experience that they have for each and every competency, using the following scale:

- Y1 — Very strong experience in the competency

- Y2 — Good experience in the competency

- Y3 — Some experience in the competency

- N — No experience in the competency

To gain total clarity on their answers, I also ask candidates to write down WHY they grade themselves as they do. I tell them that I am not asking for their theories or thoughts about a criterion, but to describe specifically what level of DIRECT experience they have to justify their answer. When and where did they have the experience? What happened?

Asking candidates to fill out this Experience Matrix is invaluable. Besides getting information beyond their resume so you can start making some determinations, these candidate responses can tell you several additional interesting things:

1. Are the candidates realistic in how well they know their own strengths and weaknesses, which speaks to their Emotional Intelligence?

2. Did they rate themselves a Y1 for every competency? Really? Are they trying to snow you?

3. What areas do they see themselves weak in? Everyone has some soft spots. Are those areas meaningful deficits to the job?

For a high executive-level position, I am looking for an honest, realistic self-assessment. A confident, well-adjusted, emotionally intelligent executive knows and recognizes where they may be soft. They need to know those weaknesses so when they form or reshuffle their own management team, they can compensate for these soft spots via other members of their team.

I also look at the amount of effort that was put into filling out this document. I believe that it should take about an hour to do a good job. If a candidate is not willing to do that, why not? Not much interest? Not much of a story? Perhaps a bit lazy or superficial? Any of these is not a good sign.

You can find an example of an Experience Matrix in Appendix B.

Asking for Compensation History

At this time, I also ask candidates to provide me with a three-year history of their compensation, including salary, target bonus / bonus paid, stock grants and/or options—really everything, not just their current compensation. I don't want to waste anybody's time, including my own, by spending effort with a candidate who is way above and not even close to the position's compensation bandwidth, or conversely whose compensation level may indicate that they are too "light" for the position despite all their stated accomplishments.

With a complete three-year compensation history, additional questions may arise. You may notice that the compensation went up or down significantly. Why? What caused or justified the bonuses paid in that time period? How were they determined? There is a lot of possible information in this simple set of numbers that you can probe during the next phase, the interview, as I will discuss next.

"We have an opening for a square peg in a round hole."

Chapter 6

The Smart Interview Process

O NCE I HAVE the above written information from the candidate — the resume, the self-graded Experience Matrix, and the three-year compensation history — I am able to narrow down the list of candidates to a small group with whom I want to speak. I have read somewhere that interviewing is only 14% accurate in predicting a successful hire, but it needs to be done. So, here's my advice on how to make interviewing as effective as possible.

The Phone Interview

I prefer a phone conversation rather than a SKYPE call with video. Call me old-fashioned, but I think there are good reasons to not have a visual of the person at this point in time.

It is believed, and I agree, that physical appearance affects how you react to people. I don't want to be swayed, positively or negatively, at this point in the process, by anything except how the candidate compares to the pre-determined qualification specifications of the position.

I begin the phone interview by going over the Experience Matrix with the candidate. This makes it clear that I want to be efficient and discuss actual experience. I ask them to tell me why they graded themselves the way they did, giving me factual information and metrics, line item by line item, in support of their grades. I usually play "devil's advocate," pushing the candidate to further explain or even defend their self-grading until I am satisfied with the answer, one way or the other. If I detect no real examples of experience, no facts, no true track record of results relative to the specific competence, the candidate will most probably be eliminated from further consideration. Perhaps the person is not as results-oriented as I am looking for.

Sure, preparing the Experience Matrix for the phone interview takes a little extra effort on behalf of the candidate, but what is wrong with that? Both you and the candidate should equally want to confirm that the match is optimal, and that there is mutually beneficial alignment between the candidate and the position. Any process that meaningfully helps in that regard has value. I have found, in fact, that candidates will often compliment me on this process and its thoroughness. It helps them understand how tight of an experience-based fit they might be to the position. I have had candidates tell me after going through this exercise that they themselves don't think that they are a good fit for the position, and so they remove themselves from consideration. This is refreshing honesty, and it saves everyone time and money, not to mention reducing the chance of making a hiring mistake.

This technique allows me to be very focused and time efficient, as the written information from the Experience Matrix becomes the basis for an informative interview. Finally, I believe the exercise of letting a candidate evaluate themselves backed up with supportive information, and challenging them further about the details, is very effective in getting all of the relevant data out on the table during the interview.

Grading the Candidates

As I interview the candidates, regardless how they may have graded themselves on the Experience Matrix, I will make up my own mind on a final grade to assign them relative to how they compare to each technical fit criterion the company has pre-determined for the position. The candidate's self-evaluation has been the starting point, but as we talk, I often find good reason to revise their own Y1, Y2, Y3, or N grading based on their answers to my questions. Sometimes the grade will come down if the candidate appears to have inflated his or her experience, but there are times when I am surprised that the candidate has been too modest and I up their score.

At the end of the interviews, it is my grades that count and that I use in presenting the top candidates to the client. To refresh your memory, this is the grading system that I use:

- Y1 — Very strong experience in the competency
- Y2 — Good experience in the competency
- Y3 — Some experience in the competency
- N — No experience in the competency

As mentioned, I suggested that you divide your list of experience-based competencies into two categories: Must Haves and Preferred. Here is my rule on how to decide which candidates to select as finalists following the interviews and any revised determination of their Experience Matrix grades:

- For "Must-Have" competencies, the candidate must have Y1 or Y2 experience scores on every criterion to be a finalist. Any Y3 or N scores simply eliminate that candidate from consideration. Why would you be willing to accept a candidate with only some experience or no experience for a critical competency?

- For Preferred competencies, Y1 and Y2 scores are great, but Y3 and N scores are not automatic eliminators. It depends on the specific competency in question.

Example of Candidate Grading

Let's take a look at a few examples as to how a hypothetical candidate, Sally Warren, might be scored given her grading after my interview with her. Let's say she is applying for a VP Sales position in a data network company.

EXPERIENCE CRITERIA	GRADE
Industry Relevance	
• **PRIMARY** Selling network data network solutions to **electric utilities**	**Y3**
• **SECONDARY** Selling network data network solutions to **utilities or municipalities**	**Y2**
• **TERTIARY** Selling **any type of network solutions** to utilities or municipalities	**Y1**
Required Experience	
• Seven or more years in a sales leadership position	**Y1**
• 10% + YOY revenue growth over past 3 years	**Y2**
• Selling solutions with deal size of $1MM+	**Y2**
• Direct selling vs. through distributor/independent representatives	**Y1**
Preferred Experience	
• Selling transmission/distribution services vs. generation	**Y3**
• Experience with CRM software	**Y1**
• In a mid-sized company	**N**

In my assessment of this candidate, I would say that Ms. Warren looks pretty good from an experience-based point of view, though not perfect. She has strong TERTIARY industry experience, good SECONDARY industry experience but only some PRIMARY industry experience. She could be stronger in that regard, but she is in the ballpark. She has been in a sales leadership role longer than my client actually wanted. Her sales revenue growth track record has been good, but below the rather aggressive requirement of the client (6% YOY vs.

the client's 10% YOY). She has good experience selling larger deals (60% of her deals sold were $1MM+), but to get a Y1 grade in that experience competency, for example, I would want 80%+ over $1MM. And, finally her experience has been entirely in direct selling, not through third-party channels.

There were a couple issues on the preferred competencies. She had only worked for large companies, and there is always a concern whether a candidate from a very large company can be as effective in a smaller company where the sales support services may not be as strong; and she came primarily from the generation side of the business. But, these experience competencies were preferred, not "must-haves."

Contribution-Centric Interviewing

Another technique that I employ in the phone conversation is what I call Contribution-Centric interviewing. The goal is to get at the specific contributions the candidate made to prior positions. For example, I would say, "You went into this position on January 1, 2014 (for example). You left the position on September 1, 2017" (or perhaps the candidate is still in the position). Then I would ask questions such as:

- What were the specific criteria that you were evaluated on (and I want the candidate to give me actual metric-based criteria, not generalizations)?

- What were those metrics when you started (current, rolling 12, whatever is relevant)?

- What are those metrics now (or when you left the position)?

- What happened and why? Was there improvement in these metrics? How much? If not, why not? What role did you play to achieve these results? If you are looking for an executive who can **lead** and drive results, and the candidate was involved in achieving the stated results but was **not** the prime mover, she may not be your true Value-Builder.

These questions allow you to dissect a candidate's stated accomplishments. I don't go further than five years back in time, as beyond that is dated and really doesn't add a lot of value in my view. We need to know what have been their recent accomplishments. I keep asking for examples using this string of questions until I am satisfied that I really understand the actual accomplishments of the candidate.

Interviewing about Soft Skills

Once you have gone through the evaluation of the Experience Matrix, you can usually open up the conversation to probe on the softer traits and behaviors you want to know about the person relative to the Personal and Cultural Fit perspectives. Remember that you will also be administering to finalist candidates the psychological assessments that more accurately measure these characteristics, but during your conversation, you can do some preliminary verbal inquiry to form an initial subjective opinion.

When interviewing for soft skills, refrain from asking non-specific open-ended questions. These are useless, for both you and the candidate. For example, a CEO client of mine once interviewed a candidate for an SVP, Supply Chain who would report directly to him. He told me he believed he only needed to ask one question: "So, tell me about yourself." Really? As if that will produce valuable information?

The best type of questions for interviewing about soft skills are behavioral questions. So rather than ask, *Do you consider yourself a good team player and why?*, which is an opinion question, say, *Tell me about a time when you were part of a team, what role you played, and how it worked out.* This is a behavioral question, because the answer should include specific behavior the candidate took to accomplish a goal.

You can find a comprehensive list of behavioral questions organized by subject matter in Appendix C.

Crossing Your "t's" and Dotting Your "i's"

Once you have interviewed all the candidates of interest, you can make a comparative analysis that allows you to assess the strength of their technical qualifications against the competency criteria, as well as comparing candidates to each other. Not surprisingly, the top candidates will usually jump right out at this point.

Before taking their time and yours to have them take the assessments, I suggest you ask these finalists to provide you with several additional documents, information, and consents, so that there are no surprises. These include:

- A signed **Statement of Truth** attesting that all information they have provided has been truthful to the best of their knowledge. In the event that someone has had the nerve to lie about their past, you have at least asked them directly about their truthfulness. Fortunately, these sorts of misrepresentations seldom happen at the executive level, but we all have heard of those inexplicable rare cases of executives who pad their resume and experience with fake information and/or accomplishments.

- A signed **Educational Credential Consent** form giving you permission to confirm the educational degrees they claim to have. I ask for this for every candidate I want to present to a client. If a candidate is going to "puff up" their credentials, this is a common area.

- A signed **Background Check Consent** form. Your company may or may not do this routinely, but if not, it should be considered. You should use a third-party firm whose business is to conduct background checks. Note that you are only asking for the candidate's consent at this time. You can decide later in the process whether you will conduct a full background check. But if they don't want to give their consent to you, why not? That should be a red flag to you and you need to find out why. If their rationale seems weak, you need to re-visit if that candidate should remain a finalist. For any financial position, however, you **must** conduct a professional background check to ensure the candidate has an impeccably clean record with no financial improprieties.

- I also ask candidates to give me a **Job Change Explanation**—a short, written statement as to the dynamics of each job or career move they have made. Sometimes these explanations are obvious and sufficient, but sometimes they can raise additional questions you will want to discuss further with the candidate. Either way, it is valuable information. Every client that I have wants to understand the why's of a candidate's career path.

- And finally, a written recognition that **Relocation is Required,** if it is. I have seen candidates try to bypass this issue by thinking that if a client falls in love with them, that they can make relocation a negotiable item.

"Sorry Mr. Arbutnot, I'm not interested."

Chapter 7

Conducting Scientific
Assessments on the Finalists

O NCE YOUR INITIAL slate of finalists is selected, you
can invite the leading candidates to take any series
of personality assessments you have decided to use.
Assessing a candidate's Personal and Cultural Fit is the perfect area where scientifically-based assessment tools can play
a significant role in understanding how well someone aligns
with the specific job and the company culture. Today, many
key elements of someone's personality can be measured in
very meaningful ways using psychological assessment tools
that are accurately predictive. These measurement tools,
while not infallible, are quite perceptive and can help you
understand a candidate's strengths and weakness, thinking
style, and ability to fit into your culture—and whether there

is a close alignment in all these areas between the candidate and the specific position.

Again, it is up to you to determine which assessments to administer and from which firms. The Hogan assessments, which I use, measure around 35 individual elements or types of behavior in a battery of four online assessments that take about twenty minutes each to complete. Again, there are other companies that offer these types of assessment tools, so it is your choice.

Establishing Your Own Contextual Standards

Before I describe the assessment tools I use, let me emphasize that, no matter which company's assessment tools you choose to employ, you must begin by understanding what each item to be assessed means, individual measurement by individual measurement. Then, for each one, you need to pre-determine and establish a standard and baseline score, reflecting what you want in a candidate. Just as you need to do this for Technical Fit, you need to create your own standards for the Personal and Cultural Fits.

When I help my clients establish these standards, it requires self-reflection and a discussion about each criterion. There is no "right answer" per se in these assessments; it depends on what you believe is needed for the job. You may find yourself debating the optimal score or range of scores you would like for each characteristic or quality. But when you are done, you will have defined a complete context that you believe describes the type of person best suited—both personally and culturally—to generate top performance in the position to be filled. I have a format that I have developed to help my clients set their standards. It usually only takes about one hour to get these standards established.

Let me give you some examples. Take the personal quality or characteristic called ADJUSTMENT, which the Hogan and many other assessments will measure. This behavioral characteristic has to do with the degree to which a person is calm, composed, even-tempered. The assessment scoring ranges from 1 (Low) to 100 (High) points or percentiles. As a normal curve would predict, most individuals fall within the middle range, and that may be what you want. But let's say you decide you need someone who is outside the norm or average for a specific characteristic.

Adjustment	Positive Behaviors	Negative Behaviors
High Score (80+)	Very calm/consistent	Unwilling to be self-critical
	Handles stress/pressure well	Ignores negative feedback
	Self-confident	Will not take advice
	Even-tempered/upbeat	Acts indifferent to deadlines
	Adapts well to change	Seems arrogant
Adjustment	Positive Behaviors	Negative Behaviors
Low Score (<20)	Emotionally expressive	Tense & self-critical
	Candid & honest	Moody & temperamental
	Self-aware	Worrisome & stress prone
	Open to feedback	Easily irritated with others
	Shows a sense of urgency	Defensive about work
	Diligent	Takes criticism personally

How would you use their assessment results? What would high or low scores mean about the individual? It turns out the both high and low scores bring some very positive behaviors, but they also suggest some negative behaviors you may not want.

In the chart on page 69, compare the positive behaviors for the High Scores to the positive behaviors of Low Scores. Which is the "better" way to be, given the position to be filled? In terms of the element of ADJUSTMENT, which will drive value-building performance in that specific position?

Now also compare the negative behaviors. Which behaviors might pose more risks to you if a candidate has either a very high or low score?

Another personal quality or characteristic that I look at is called INQUISITIVE. It has to do with imagination, curiosity, and creative potential. There are pros and cons in terms of behaviors for both high and low scores here, too.

Inquisitive	Positive Behaviors	Negative Behaviors
High Score (80+)	Imaginative & creative	Overanalyzes problems
	Bright & inventive	Difficulty in making decisions
	Quick-witted	Impractical
	Understands the big picture	Can become bored
	Open to change	Impatient with details
	Interested in new ideas	Poor implementer
	Thinks strategically	Lack of tolerance for the routine

Inquisitive	Positive Behaviors	Negative Behaviors
Low Scores (<20)	Follows rules & procedures	Lacks imagination
	Very focused interests	Resists innovation
	Tolerates routine tasks	Has a narrow perspective
	Not easily bored	Ignores the big picture
	Can focus on details	Uncomfortable with ambiguity

Compare the negative behaviors for the High Scores to the negative behaviors of Low Scores. Which is the "worse" way to be? Well, what does your position call for? In terms of the elements of INQUISITIVE, what will drive performance in the specific position?

Determining Standards Is More Challenging Than You Think

Here's the point: Setting your standards is not as simple as you might think. You can't just say you want 100 on every measurement. A score of 100 is not necessarily better than a score of 20 in certain types of positions! There are positive and negative behaviors for every score, which manifest themselves in the person's behavior and hence performance. Therefore, the question becomes: *What score or range is optimal for that position, in your culture?*

In effect, you need to understand the significance of each measurement on any psychological profiling assessment tool you choose to use. What do the range of scores mean? What behaviors are associated with the scoring scale? Which score works best for the position you are hiring? A comparative context is critical. There are degrees of any personal quality, and each degree has positives and negatives about it.

You therefore need to reflect in advance as to what type and degree of personality, and therefore behavior, best suits the position and make a judgment as to what blend of qualities are needed. This will determine where on the spectrum the various types of personal characteristics have to score to drive strong performance and value creation in your SPECIFIC position. If you can't define exactly what you need for a Value-Builder, or at least come as close as possible, how in the world will you find him or her? Pure luck?

For instance, here's an example using our hypothetical candidate Sally Warren for the two elements just discussed compared to the standards set by the client.

Personal Competency	Client Standard	Warren	Alignment
Adjustment	70–85	69	No
Inquisitive	60–80	62	Yes

In this executive search for an SVP, Marketing & Sales, let's say that the client and I decided that the ADJUSTMENT range needed to be at 70-85, given that a Sales Leader does need confidence, resilience, etc., but not be so high as to possibly be conceited, arrogant and/or too full of themselves.

And while this candidate was not in alignment, she was a near miss at a 69 percentile.

But imagine if Ms. Warren's ADJUSTMENT score was a 15 percentile. That is a meaningful misalignment and there would be consequences. That gap could very well negatively affect her performance.

However, regarding INQUISITIVE, we didn't want a candidate who was simply practical or highly detail oriented, who would usually favor the tried and true over new ideas, and be narrow in their perspective. There is nothing wrong with being that way, but this position called for some creativity, new ideas, and an openness to try new things. The INQUISITVE standard range was thus set at 60–80. The client wanted above the median of 50 but not so high that some negative behaviors could get in the way of performance. Candidate Warren scored a 62 percentile, in alignment on the low side, but a Yes.

So, to summarize, these are the steps to using assessment tools in an effective way.

1. List what each assessment measures, and understand what the elements to be measured mean. Understand what the range of scores means in terms of both positive and negative behaviors.

2. Determine where on each characteristic's measurement scale you believe is the type of personality/behavior that will drive results. Set a range for that metric standard that you will be seeking in a candidate.

3. Have each candidate complete the assessment.

4. Analyze the degree of alignment or misalignment
    between each candidate's results and the standards
    you are seeking.

    Let me now review how I use the various assessments.

Personal (Position/Job) Alignment

Measuring and understanding personality/behavior is a must,
in my view. Personality drives behavior, and at the end of the
day, that behavior will literally drive business unit performance. I view the link between personality and performance
as a chain that connects them as follows:

**PERSONALITY ➜ BEHAVIOR/VALUES/CRITICAL THINKING ➜
LEADERSHIP STYLE ➜ TEAM ENGAGEMENT / COMMITMENT
➜ BUSINESS UNIT PERFORMANCE**

Scientific assessments such as Hogan's aim to assess
deeply ingrained behavioral characteristics and how they
impact an individual's approach to work and interaction with
others. For example, if your personality is assertive, you will
act and be assertive.

Using precise assessment tools gives you the ability to
understand a wide range of key personal characteristics such as
leadership qualities, resilience, frankness, drive, energy, team
orientation, directedness, dependability, attitudes towards
risk taking, optimism, self-confidence, flexibility, and more.

This is invaluable information to help you make a judgment as the results of this test give you critical insights into the candidate. When you compare the measurements to the range you are looking for, you can see how closely the person aligns with your needs.

Derailment Assessment—When a Business Leader is Under Stress

Under pressure or when facing a very difficult business challenge, people may change. Their behavior under normal circumstances may get results, but when under stress, they may process information differently, treat others differently, change their decision-making process, or take actions that can demotivate co-workers. Behavioral tendencies under stress can impede success. These are called derailers! Performance strengths can cross the line to become performance weaknesses, and a major barrier to Value-Building performance.

For example, when I was a CEO, I had an executive reporting to me who was charming, energetic, bright, and engaging. But under pressure, he became Mr. Hyde to his Dr. Jekyll—moody, inconsistent, volatile, and unpredictable. It was horrible. He was single-handedly destroying morale. People were scared of him. It was a significant problem. I hadn't hired him, as he came with a company that I had purchased. But, in the end, I had to terminate him and replace him.

Here's something to think about. Consider how damaging it would be if your specific position were filled by someone who, under pressure or uncomfortable circumstances, went from one side of the spectrum described on the left (a perceived strength) to the spectrum on the right (a problem):

- Intense and energetic ... to ➔ moody, inconsistent, volatile, unpredictable

- Perceptive and insightful ... to ➔ cynical, negative, distrustful, fault-finding

- Careful and thoughtful ... to ➔ risk-averse, overly careful, and fearful of failure

- Independent and objective ... to ➔ socially withdrawn, tough, uncommunicative

- Confident and assertive ... to ➔ entitled, arrogant, overestimates their competency

- Outgoing and socially skilled ... to ➔ attention-seeking, self-promoting, dramatic

- Innovative and creative ... to ➔ eccentric, impractical, lacking focus

- Detailed and conscientious ... to ➔ micromanaging, perfectionistic, nitpicky

- Supportive and loyal ... to➔ overeager to please, deferential, ingratiating

In any company, there will always be pressure, at times quite serious. And people will always have their quirks. No one is perfect. Having some derailing tendencies is normal.

But how many are too many? Which are most dangerous to the specific position? What impact, specifically, will a derailer have on the individual's ability to perform? Will the company's performance suffer?

You should try to understand derailers BEFORE you hire someone, don't you think?! That's why I also use the Hogan assessment that measures derailment tendencies, assigning a risk factor to each. Here again, you must also pre-determine what type and how many high risk derailers you are willing to tolerate.

Business Reasoning and Critical Thinking Alignment

Another personality element that can be measured using scientific assessments is someone's thinking style. This is a key area of the personal portfolio of skills—called cognitive abilities. In fact, candidates ask me all the time, what is the "hot button" for my client for whom they are interviewing? For one client, for example, the answer was very clear and straightforward—they put a premium on critical thinking.

Again, just as with the Personal behavior qualities, before you give candidates a cognitive assessment, you have to establish a baseline range for the type of thinking needed for the position. Are the critical opportunities and/or challenges for strong performance in the specific position, in your company, within your team of executives more strategic or tactical in nature? Or is there a blend of strategic and tactical thinking needed to create strong performance and value creation in this position?

Please note that I have found that someone who is a strong strategic thinker is more upwardly mobile, as strategic thinking abilities become more important as you climb the corporate ladder. So, if upward mobility is important to this position, this assessment becomes even more useful to you.

To get at cognitive thinking style, I use several state-of-the-art assessment solutions, such as the Watson-Glaser® Assessment of Critical Thinking or the Hogan® Business Reasoning Inventory. Either of these assessments can help you evaluate how a person solves problems and what type of thinking style he or she uses. You may have already garnered some insights about a candidate's thinking abilities from the Experience Matrix and Contribution-Centric interviewing, but in my experience, these scientific tools offer more objective and therefore valuable insight that can help you judge whether a candidate is the type of thinker you need.

Cultural (Organizational) Alignment

I was once retained to recruit and place a VP Sales & Business Development for a $150MM manufacturing company. The incumbent had not been very effective in the job, and the company's top line had been flat for the last several years. In discussions with the client CEO, he identified the type of person they were seeking. It was a pretty typical job description for a VP Sales type—someone who could push the top line up, figure out some unique selling propositions, and segment the markets to be served more effectively to grow the business.

After laying out the Technical and Personal Fit criteria, I took him through the format to define the company culture and we established some standards. It was just the CEO and I who went through this exercise, so I took everything at his word.

Soon, I found and presented some candidates, one of whom the client fell in love with. He was in fact a dynamic sales leader. He was a positive go-getter who had the confidence and courage to install changes that would improve the business. The CEO hired him, and everyone was thrilled — for a while.

But in this case, it was not my candidate who caused a problem. As I later learned, the company had, shall we say, a "difficult" culture. It was fraught with fear as the CEO was, to put it mildly, "single-minded." He refused any ideas other than his own, and blamed others when things went wrong. He undermined his direct reports. Everyone took sides against the other. It was a rough and tumble toxic environment. The CEO had misrepresented the culture. Rather than defining what the culture was, he had described the culture he wanted, or he did not understand what the environment was that his behavior created, or perhaps he was just too embarrassed to admit it to an outsider.

As a result of the culture, the formidable skills of the hired candidate could not be effectively employed. Continually undermined, the new VP became extremely frustrated as he was dragged down by barriers put in front of any new sales initiatives he proposed. The company simply didn't know, or would not admit, what their situation was, or what the motivational infrastructure of their culture was. As a result, an otherwise very capable candidate did not fit into it, and failed.

I am not passing judgment on that culture. I am just saying that you must truthfully define your culture, the good and bad of it, to find an effective fit. This VP's failure didn't have to occur. Some people are just more effective than others in such a difficult environment; i.e., they are more resilient and less sensitive. If I had known the actual situation at that company, I would have found a much better fit in a person who could deal with these types of cultural conflicts and still be highly effective.

Today, when I am taking a client through the questionnaire to define their company culture, I much prefer that the information and opinions not come exclusively from the CEO. I suggest that several other executives be involved in the discussion, as I have found that a CEO may not fully understand what is going on "beneath" him or her. In the case just discussed, I relaxed a bit on that policy, which I usually follow, and I learned my lesson.

As this story shows, it is essential that you examine your culture and understand it. How does your culture motivate people? What specific behaviors within the culture of the company result in a promotion, higher bonuses, recognition, etc.?

Of course, every organization has a unique culture with "issues" of some kind. But, regardless of whatever cultural issues you have, you always need to find someone who can deliver results and work within them. If the alignment is not strong, the culture will create hurdles and barriers to the candidate's ability to perform at a high level, and you will not see their top performance. Frustration will follow and results will be even further affected. Why take the chance?

As with the other areas of the CompleteFIT, you thus need to assess your culture and honestly admit to the type of Cultural Fit you should seek between the company and new executive hire. Consider questions like these:

- Does your culture value progress, diversity, autonomy . . . or role clarity and conservatism?

- Does your culture value experience-based, intuitive decisions . . . or analytics and data-driven decision-making?

- Does your culture value risk-taking and experimentation . . . or structure, order, and predictability?

- Does your culture value cooperation and consensus . . . or top-down authority and decision-making?

- Does your culture value work-life balance, collaboration, and cooperation . . . or individual results, making money, a strong focus on the bottom line while all else is secondary?

- Does your culture value public acknowledgement and visibility . . . or behind-the-scenes recognition and team acknowledgement?

- Does your culture value self-reliance and personal responsibility . . . or teamwork, mentoring, and helping others?

Example of a Cultural Assessment

Let's look at a specific example of a motivational quality or characteristic that may determine cultural alignment. Take AFFILIATION, which refers to whether being "affiliated," part of something, motivates a person.

A high score (> 80 percentile) would indicate that the candidate highly values:

- Working with others

- Teamwork

- Leading a team

- Recognition of the team over the individual

- Being visible

- Social interaction

- Consensus

- Commitment

Conversely, a low score (< 20 percentile) would indicate that the candidate highly values:

- Working alone

- Individual contribution

- Individual recognition

- A task-oriented environment

- A more formal environment

- Taking the lead as an individual

Which does your company culture value? One or the other, or a blend? While this may vary somewhat by the specific position, there is usually an overriding attitude in a company culture that you can identify and define.

I am often told by a CEO, "Well, I would like to change our culture and make it more X or Y...." How better to do that than to hire executives whose motivational profiles are in alignment with the desired change in culture? A word of warning however: if you hire a change-maker, you need to support and stand behind the new executive as the changes try to gain traction. It won't work otherwise.

Scoring Candidates on Cultural Fit

I have a format to help my clients define the motivation infrastructure of their organization and set the contextual standards. It is a similar process to setting the desired standards for Personal (position/job) Fit discussed above.

With the Hogan assessments, I can measure ten motivational elements, of which AFFILIATION is just one. Other tests may measure a different number of motivational charac-teristics, but the value of the assessment is still unquestion-able. Then, using a 100-point scale, I work with the client to determine what type of candidate profile is needed for a strong motivational/cultural alignment on each element.

We can then use a scientific assessment tool to determine the motivational profile of a candidate and to what degree that is in alignment with the motivational infrastructure of the company. Will the candidate fit into the culture? Or will he or she be constantly swimming against the current?

To create an overall evaluation of candidates who have taken the assessment, I calculate a variance between the desired scoring and the candidate's scoring. Based on the size of the variance, I can determine whether the alignment is Strong, Good, Average, or Weak. For instance, let's say the client's desired standard is 70 on one of the criterion. If the candidate scored a 45 percentile, the variance would be 25; if a candidate scored a 60, the variance is just 10.

Using the degree of variance, I then assign a category to each measure for the candidate, as follows.

- Strong Alignment — Variance of <10
- Good Alignment — Variance of 11 to 25
- Average Alignment — Variance of 26 to 40
- Weak Alignment — Variance of > 40

If I see more than three Weak Alignments in a candi-date, I will almost always eliminate the person from further consideration. That's how important cultural alignment is, in my view. A greater than 40-point deviation from the client's standards means that the candidate simply may not fit very well into that element of the culture. The more alignments in the Strong category, the better fit it will be!

Ethical (Business Values) Alignment

A CEO once told me:

1. I interview based on skill!

2. I hire based on fit!

3. I promote based on performance!

4. I fire based on character!

I could not agree more with this CEO that an executive's character as expressed in the person's ethical values must be considered in the hiring process. Admittedly, ethics are a difficult item to measure. I know of no direct assessment tool that can definitively predict a person's ethics. However, there are ways to get at assessing ethical values.

For example, I provide candidates with several problematic real-life business scenarios and ask them to write out what they would do in each situation. These are subtle dilemmas that force one to think about choices to be made and which values must guide a decision. Here are some examples:

1. Our food company has a QC policy of holding all products for 24 hours after they come off

the production line before shipping them to our customers. We have never had a QC problem that required us not to ship. However, our largest customer, who hates late shipments, has a truck on our lot waiting to be loaded and taken away. The products have not reached the 24-hour mark yet. The buyer is calling, threatening to pull the business. What should you do?

2. A fellow employee (and friend) has told you that he/she plans to quit the company in two months and start a new job that was offered to him/her by one of our fiercest competitors. What should you do?

I have numerous such subtle universal business scenarios that are germane to any executive position, all geared to surfacing the ethical thinking and value system of a candidate. Sometimes the candidate's answers are black and white, a definite "I'd do X or Y." Other times, I have had candidates come up with very creative solutions. On the whole, the candidate's answers paint a pretty clear picture of how the person deals with complex decisions that pit one choice against another, with each choice indicative of an ethical value that the candidate subscribes to.

"Nice Job."

Chapter 8

Comparing Finalist Candidates

AT THE END of the process, it comes time to select a final candidate to hire, right? You have to make a choice from among the top candidates who have submitted their resumes, filled out the Experience Matrix and other documents, gone through the interviews, and taken the various assessments. So how do you make that final selection?

I find it very helpful to lay out the strengths, weaknesses and degrees of alignment/misalignment of the candidates under consideration in comparison to the established CompleteFIT standards—Technical/Experience-based, Personal and Cultural—as well as against each other.

To do this, I create a comprehensive comparative chart that uses:

- The Y1, Y2, Y3, N measurement for the technical, experience-based competencies

- The "in" or "not in alignment" scoring for the personal (job/position), derailment, and cognitive competencies

- The Strong (S), Good (G), Average (A), or Weak (W) alignment measurement for the cultural competencies

This chart is just what you'd expect—an Excel spreadsheet with columns listing the finalist candidates and rows listing all of the measurements with the grading I have given to each candidate, as well as all the predetermined standards or standard ranges.

Taking into Account Relative Price-Value Considerations

I also include each candidate's current cash compensation in the grid so as to construct a **price-value** comparison among candidates as well. What type and/or level of talent and alignment would you be getting for your human capital investment?

In general, I have always suggested that companies allow for a 15%-20% bandwidth around the targeted compensation for an executive position. For example, if the cash compensation target (salary + bonus) is $215K for a position, I believe that you should be considering candidates seeking cash compensation of $180K to $250K. This allows you to make better price-value judgments for the position in question. For instance, you may find a great candidate who is above the $215K target but who is so impressive you may not want to lose out on hiring him or her. The question then becomes: could someone making 15% above the targeted compensation be meaningfully stronger, and as such, worth the extra compensation? Conversely, if you believe that a candidate making 15% less than the targeted compensation is good enough, why not save some money?

Frankly, in every search that I have conducted, these price-value lines or delineations become remarkably clear. I always show clients a reasonable range of price-value candidate options, so they can make a good ROI-based hiring decision. I encourage you to utilize that approach as well.

Example of a Comprehensive Candidate Comparison

Here is an example of the spreadsheet I create to help with this analysis.

Let's say we have four candidates being evaluated for the position of VP Marketing. The target cash compensation has been set at $215K; $175K in salary and a $40K (20%)bonus. The next page shows the type of spreadsheet I construct to help with the analysis and comparison of candidates.

CANDIDATE COMPARISON

Current/Most Recent Cash Compensation						
		Standard	Thomas	Bain	Williams	Wilson
	Salary	$175K	$210K	$190K	$175K	$150K
	Bonus	$40K (23%)	$40K (20%)	$25K (20%)	$35K (20%)	$30K (20%)
	Total Cash Compensation	$215K	$250K	$215K	$210K	$180K

Technical/Experience-Based Alignment					
		Thomas	Bain	Williams	Wilson
Industry Relevance	Primary	N	Y2	Y3	Y1
	Secondary	Y3	Y2	Y2	Y1
	Tertiary	Y1	Y2	Y2	Y1
	Total Y1 or Y2	**1**	**3**	**2**	**3**
Required Competencies	Y1	5	3	2	2
	Y2	2	4	5	5
	Y3	0	0	0	0
	N	0	0	0	0
	Total Y1 or Y2	**7**	**7**	**7**	**7**
Preferred Competencies	Y1	1	1	2	0
	Y2	3	2	2	2
	Y3	1	1	1	3
	N	0	1	0	0
	Total Y1 or Y2	**4**	**3**	**4**	**2**
High Risk Derailers [≤ 2]		0	2	1	4

Cognitive Alignment				
	Thomas	Bain	Williams	Wilson
In Alignment	1	3	2	1
Not In Alignment-High	2	0	0	1
Not in Alignment-Low	0	0	1	1

Personal (Job/Position) Alignment				
	Thomas	Bain	Williams	Wilson
In Alignment	3	5	2	1
Not In Alignment-High	3	0	1	3
Not in Alignment-Low	1	2	4	3

Cultural (Organizational) Alignment				
	Thomas	Bain	Williams	Wilson
Strong	4	5	4	5
Good	3	2	3	4
Average	3	3	3	1
Weak	0	0	0	0
Total Strong/Good	**7**	**7**	**7**	**9**

Education					
		Thomas	Bain	Williams	Wilson
Required	BA/BS in a Business Discipline	**Yes**	**Yes**	**Yes**	**Yes**
Preferred	MBA	**Yes**	No	No	**Yes**

This comparison chart offers a summary and detailed analysis of each candidate in terms of:

1. Their degree of industry relevance

2. Their strength of experience for the required experience-based competencies

3. Their strength of experience for the preferred experience-based competencies

4. Their number of high risk performance derailing tendencies

5. Their degree of alignment for the cognitive standards as set by the client

6. Their degree of alignment for the personal standards as set by the client

7. Their degree of alignment for the cultural standards as set by the client

All these measures are presented in the context of their total cash compensation. Of course, you can use this approach utilizing the candidate's salary rather than cash compensation.

Let's study this example. First, we can see that candidate Wilson clearly has the strongest degree of industry relevancy, with PRIMARY industry experience (she works for a direct competitor). And she is the "cheapest" of the four candidates. As it is my presentation policy, all four of the candidates have been graded a Y1 or Y2 in the required competencies. But Wilson is the weakest in terms of Y1-level strength and degree of experience for both the required and preferred competencies as compared to the other candidates who have higher numbers. Her personal alignment is also not as good as the others; while her cultural alignment is on par with them. In fact, the cultural alignment of all four candidates is about the same. She does have four high-risk derailers; more than the other three candidates and above the norm. Conventional wisdom might say that a candidate with direct industry experience and who is at the lower end of the acceptable compensation bandwidth would be the best bet. Let's not be so sure.

In comparison, candidate Thomas would appear in many ways to be the strongest candidate in terms of the desired competencies although his industry experience relevancy, while within the desired concentric circles, is the weakest. His industry relevancy is only Tertiary. But the strength and degree of his experience for the required competencies is meaningfully higher than the other candidates. And he has no high-risk performance derailing tendencies. His personal alignment is good but not the best of the four. But he is the most expensive of the candidates. Is he worth the extra investment?

Candidate Bain is an interesting candidate. Right on the cash compensation target, stronger in the required competencies than Wilson, but not as strong as Thomas. She has SECONDARY industry relevancy experience. And, she is very well aligned with the position from a personal fit perspective, the strongest of the four! She has two high-risk derailers, which is the norm.

That leaves candidate Williams, at least at this point in the search, who would cost you about the same as Bain. He has the second least amount of PRIMARY industry experience (but again, enough to be of interest) and only one high risk derailer. His Y1 scores on the required and preferred competencies are slightly below Bain, but better than the cheaper Wilson. And, he ranks third in terms of personal alignment.

As you can see, this analytical approach allows you to make a detailed comparison between the candidates, examining them in terms of your criteria and standards to assess how they align from a CompleteFIT perspective. Such a comparative analysis of the candidates gives you an effective overview, but it also allows you to go to a more detailed level of decision-making information, given that not all the criteria are equal in terms of importance to you. You can boost the criteria and competencies that are most important to you and discount those that are less so, to make this analysis even more useful.

In the end, this informational grid allows both my client and me to identify the candidate(s) who most closely align with the blend of experience and competencies needed for value-building performance in the job as the client defined them, and who offer the best price-value option.

If you cannot decide on whether or who to hire at this point, and you feel a need to continue to recruit, assess, and consider future candidates, this grid is an efficient tool. You simply remove candidates that have been eliminated from consideration from the grid, then add any new candidates that have emerged for comparison with the remaining potential candidates. In this way, you always have a thorough, holistic, up-to-date chart of all candidates under consideration.

At the end of the process, the candidate that compares and aligns the most favorably to the elements of comparison that are the most important to you is most likely your CompleteFIT choice. That candidate will have the range and blend of the necessary competencies to increase your company's value.

Ranking the Candidates in the Example

Given all of the factors that we have just reviewed, how would you rank these four VP Marketing candidates? Who do you think should be the preferred candidate? That final determination is entirely up to you, as it depends on your priorities.

Do you want to know how I would rank the candidates? I would be more than happy to lay out my ranking and the reasons for that ranking for your consideration. But that will take a short discussion. So, please email me at wle@edwards-search.com and we can set up a short phone call to discuss.

Putting the Art and Science of Recruiting Together

I stated earlier in the book that I agree that recruiting is both an art and a science. While I have emphasized the critical value of using proven psychological assessment tools as a scientific element in evaluating candidates, I must add that you may need to merge back in the art of hiring when you are making your final choice.

While the assessment tools provide valuable data points in selecting your final candidate and having confidence that he or she can deliver the strong business performance you expect, I do not want to suggest that these assessment tools are the be-all and end-all in terms of assessing a candidate's ability to perform. In other words, you should not allow a couple of "bad" test results to become a deal breaker if the candidate has nearly everything else you seek.

"It's the perfect job if self-respect isn't a factor."

Chapter 9

Making the Hire: References, Making the Offer, and Onboarding

N OW THAT YOU have selected your candidate of choice, it's time for the next phase of hiring — the checking of candidate references, the offer of employment, and assisting the hiree to transition into your company. Allow me to offer my thoughts on how these steps work best.

Checking Candidate References and Background

While checking a candidate's professional references may or may not provide valuable information in your final decision-making, I highly recommend that it be done before you finalize the hiring. The best references by a long shot are the candidate's former bosses — the more recent the better. These people can offer their thoughts from the same vantage point that you will have, as the individual's boss. So whenever possible, they are worth speaking to.

Of course, there are times when a candidate is still employed and has gone through the job search in stealth mode. You clearly cannot ask them to reveal their interest in another job by asking to speak to their current boss. In that case, you should not do anything that may put the candidate in jeopardy.

When I do call references, I probe about SPECIFC information gaps about the candidate or any residual areas I may have of concern as a result of what I have learned in the assessment and conversation process. I ask very pointed questions, so I can better understand the candidate's technical strengths and weaknesses, personal quirks, and motivational drivers. No softball or generalized questions like, "Tell me about Ms. Warren. What are Ms. Warren's weaknesses?" These types of questions prove useless, in my opinion.

I also try to clarify issues about the candidate that I may not be 100% certain of. This is your chance to learn final bits of information about the individual before you decide whether to make an offer.

Checking the candidate's educational credentials is a must at this time. This is an area where fluffing a bit seems to be most prevalent among candidates. I have no tolerance for any candidate who has not been 100% truthful, including that they actually received the degree they claim. Being a few credit hours short does not cut it. Almost receiving a degree is not receiving a degree. It is the principle that counts! This type of exaggeration doesn't occur often, but it does happen.

A full-fledged executive background check is also recommended. There are professional providers who conduct these checks and they really don't cost a lot to use ($500 or so). Why take chances, and better safe than sorry. This is especially true for positions of financial responsibility, where you absolutely cannot risk missing out on any issues in the candidate's background.

I once had a candidate who was made an offer for a CFO position contingent upon a satisfactory background check. The background check uncovered several DUIs. The candidate would have been much better off disclosing that information, acknowledging a problem, and explaining how it had been resolved. But he didn't, and the client would not have known about it without having done the background check. To make matters worse, the client was a large wine distribution company. That candidate was dropped like a hot potato by the client.

The Delicacies of Making the Offer

Sometimes companies may make a mistake when putting together an offer of employment to a candidate that they wish to hire. Here's an example of what I mean. I once had an assignment to fill a VP Operations position for a food manufacturer. I found, evaluated, assessed, and presented a very good candidate whom the client really liked. When it was time for an offer to be made, I provided a history of the candidate's compensation, and it was pretty clear what the offer should have looked like. However, the CEO did not ask for my input on the terms of the offer, and so she made one that was ridiculously low, embarrassingly so. What was she thinking?

The candidate was literally offended, even angry at having wasted his time. He removed himself from consideration . . . in a huff. I asked the CEO why she did that. She said she was expecting the candidate to negotiate, so she went in low to leave room to negotiate up. That was a costly and unnecessary mistake. I managed to fill the position with another candidate a month later, but to be honest, the lost candidate was better than the hired candidate, in my view.

Here's the point: I believe that companies need to make a fair offer, right from the start. I disagree with the idea of making low-ball offers in anticipation of a protracted negotiation and the possibility of saving a little money. Also, if it is not a reasonably fair offer, your professional relationship with the selected candidate may get off on a sour note. That approach only serves to illustrate that the company may be misinformed as to current market rate salaries, is overly cost sensitive, or does not really appreciate the candidate's ability to contribute as much as he or she thought you did. A strong candidate is very likely to be offended by a low-ball offer, as seen in the story above.

For this reason, I don't believe that a company and a properly vetted candidate who find it mutually beneficial to work together, and who are very excited about that happening, should let a 10%, or even 20%, compensation difference interfere with the hiring process. Everyone needs to put their "big boy" or "big girl" pants on and find a compensation package that will work for both. If nothing else, why not just split the difference?

At the same time, let me add that I also tell my candidates that a starting salary and bonus are important but should not be blown out of proportion at this early stage of their relationship. If the candidate to be hired is the optimal and CompleteFIT candidate, he or she will go in and do a top-notch job. Their performance will help increase the company's value, which will be noticed, and the money will come to the hired candidate as they prove themselves.

So, a reasonable and fair offer should work from both the client's and candidate's perspectives!

My 9.5 Rule

Let's say you have found a candidate you really like. He or she aligns very well with all the hard and soft competencies you have determined you need and want in that position. But you find yourself wondering if there may be other candidates who might be a little better, waiting to be discovered if you just look a little longer. Should you hire the in-hand current candidate, or keep looking? If you keep looking, you run the risk of losing the found candidate.

Here's my advice if you are waffling. Take all the information you have on the candidate (both subjective and objective) and using your good judgment, assign them a score on a 10-point scale. A score of 10 is the perfect candidate (who doesn't exist in my view); a score of 1 is a terrible candidate.

In my view any candidate with your rating of 8.5 or higher should be considered a "qualified" candidate. But, if you can give the candidate under consideration a 9.5 or higher, I would attempt to hire without delay. If you cannot find it in yourself to give the candidate at least a 9.5, you may indeed want to hold off and keep looking.

Of course, the issue of timing and your sense of urgency will affect this decision. If the position needs to be filled ASAP because some important activities are not getting done, this 9.5 rule is the approach to take. If you have more time to hire, you may want to keep looking. But please remember, you will most probably never find a 10! I believe **9.5** is a great score, indicating that this is the candidate for you.

The Benefits of 1-on-1 Onboarding and Mentoring

Ok, you've put out your offer and the candidate has accepted. The next step is bringing the person in and getting them started in the job. This is yet another critical juncture in the recruiting process that you need to do correctly.

A survey by The Institute of Executive Development found that the "ramp up" time for external executives in a new position is commonly six to nine months, and only 8% of those surveyed found pre-employment activities to be effective. That is why I firmly believe in helping a new executive transition into their new position using a formalized "onboarding" program. Yes, some executives don't need it, as they are emotionally intelligent enough to be able to handle the issues, pressures, and challenges of what is often a major transition in their career without any support. But in my view, many executives could benefit from some help in their early months on the job, but just won't admit it. The problem is, you don't usually know how to predict who needs some help and who does not, so I simply recommend it for everyone.

The goal of a good onboarding program is to help the transitioning executive make meaningful contributions ASAP, that is, to accelerate their assimilation into the new position and company as rapidly as can happen. The sooner that executive is paying for himself or herself as a Value-Builder, the better!

In my estimation, one of the most critical elements of successful onboarding is having a mentor — someone who has been in the type or level of position being filled (or higher) — work with the transitioning executive. Some companies offer a new executive an internal person to be the mentor. However, I don't think having an internal mentor is the way to go, because someone on the inside will not be objective and may reveal information to others in the organization that the new hire prefers to keep confidential. It is critical that the onboarding be a totally confidential process. The new executive must feel that he or she can be completely honest and open about any issues that may block their efficient assimilation into your company. Is their boss a jerk? Are colleagues uncooperative? Are the executive's direct reports resistant to following his or her leadership? Whatever the issues, the person must be able to have a private, confidential conversation with someone who can be trusted to listen objectively, not tattletale, and respond with feedback and recommendations in an equally honest way.

For this reason, I recommend that you bring in an outside professional mentor to work with the new hire one-on-one, and the best choice is someone who knows that role. A great mentor must be able to understand the challenges and responsibilities of the specific position, and work with the executive to give guidance and advice as how to not stub their toe. For example, someone who has already been a CFO or CEO/COO is better equipped to mentor and onboard a new CFO than a generic professional coach with mid-level business experience (usually HR- or OD-based), as they have had first-hand experience in what the new hire may face. The coaching community will probably cry foul at that statement, but that's my professional opinion.

The most common issue that seems to come up in the onboarding sessions that I conduct for the executives that I place is the executive's relationship with the new boss. Such problems can usually be broken down into a few key areas:

- Is communication effective between the new executive and their boss? What is the communicative style of the boss? It is the job of the new executive, not the boss, to make sure that communication is effective. The executive must "manage" to the communication style of the boss and make it work.

- Are the boss and the new executive on the same page strategically and tactically speaking? If the two of them were asked to list the short- and long-term goals for the new executive, would they cite the same list? If not, something has gone wrong and there could possibly be surprises in terms of performance evaluation later on.

- Is there agreement as to the current state of the new executive's situation? Is there a shared understanding of what resources will be needed to achieve goals, and the timing and priority of those goals?

Having a shared and mutual understanding on all these issues is critical to ensuring the new executive has every chance to become the Value-Builder you expected. But in my view, it is up to the new executive, not the boss, to ensure that these problems are resolved. No matter the issue or its level of difficulty, there are techniques that can help.

I have also found that onboarding is most effective when it is based upon the hiree's emotional intelligence. Emotional Intelligence (EQi) or Emotional Quotient (EQ) is the ability to be aware of and manage one's own and other's emotions. The new executive has to interact with others effectively as a leader and team player; with resilience, the ability to listen and reflect, impulse control, the ability to persuade, etc. As such, being emotionally intelligent is critical.

Understanding and developing emotional intelligence has multiple benefits. It allows a new executive to recognize, and even foresee, where they may be vulnerable in their transition. If you know where a landmine is, you probably won't step on it. Plus, a person's emotional intelligence can be improved, once they understand their profile and what they need to focus on. I believe there is also a correlation between emotional intelligence and upward mobility, so helping an executive improve his or her emotional intelligence can lead to increasingly higher senior leadership positions.

Additional topics for discussion with the executive during onboarding include:

- What has made the executive successful in the past? Will those qualities work in the new position as well or are there soft spots that need attention and refinement?

- How can he or she understand the culture of the new employer as quickly as possible so as to be effective and a contributor in it?

- How can he or she get some early wins to create credibility and momentum?

- What is the hired executive's learning agenda, and how might it be accelerated?

- How can lurking surprises be identified?

In the course of my years as a successful executive recruiter, I have witnessed an effective onboarding process have a meaningful positive impact on a new executive's success. I am trained as a Master Career Coach and I offer an Emotional Intelligence-based onboarding program to the executives that I place (for free), using either the Hogan EQ or Bar-On EQ-i® process. Both of these, or similar tools that measure emotional intelligence, will offer you, and more importantly the new executive, valuable information.

Using the Insights Gained about the Placed Executive

One of the benefits of using scientifically validated personality assessment tools to help in the selection process is that you can use this same information to learn how to effectively manage and motivate the newly placed executive. Here are a few examples of what I learned from the scientific assessments about a candidate who was hired by my client and that I offered to my client as another step in achieving a great placement.

- Mr. Smith is unusually self-confident. It will help to coach him to listen to others. Remind him to learn from his mistakes. Unless the role is as an individual contributor, he will need to function as an effective team player to be successful.

- Mr. Jones is very conscientious. I suggest you coach him to not micro-manage his team and to put a priority on developing his direct reports professionally. Work towards helping him become an effective delegator. Put this on the list of criteria for how you will be evaluating him.

- Ms. Harper is curious and imaginative. She could become bored with routine tasks. Be sure to continually offer her new challenges and assignments. You may be familiar with the venerated theory of people management: *Feed the lions, ride the horses, shoot the dogs!* Feed this lion.

As these examples show, any scientifically-based information you have gathered during the recruitment process can be put to use to your advantage. Help your important new hire to reach their full potential in a timely manner. You are their boss. That is your job.

"I've decided to fill the job internally.
I just don't like dealing with headhunters."

Should You Use a Recruiter?

O F COURSE, YOU should!

While I have explained my entire methodology of recruiting and hiring in this book, including the CompleteFIT process, I nevertheless want to offer my reasons for suggesting that hiring a professional recruiter to do this may be more effective for most companies.

First, for any significant investment that you make that can make a meaningful difference to your company's performance and valuation, using an expert to identify, assess, and evaluate the options — in this case, candidates — is a wise choice. Expertise matters in recruiting as much as it does in any business investment. Would you select and implement a new ERP system without some expert advice? Would you raise capital without some expert financial advice? It's the same logic. You really don't want to screw it up, and if you do, it can be very costly.

Second, if you are going to conduct a thorough search, who will handle the workload? When a client hires me, I will usually have 600-1,000 resumes pass by my eyes for a single executive search assignment. And that is just the start of what must be done. If you are searching for a Director of Finance, for example, is your CFO going to go through these hundreds of resumes, screen them for preliminary interest and further interviews, and so on? That is not what he or she was hired to do. Or will an HR manager do the screening? If so, are they really the best judge of talent for a Director of Finance (or other key executive positions) — or are they just a box checker without effective experience in assessing the competencies needed for each specific position. They probably don't even know what GAAP means.

In contrast, using a human capital expert will significantly help you in hiring the optimal candidate. A recruiter (with a background like mine as a CEO, board member, and corporate executive, for example) understands the critical challenges of executive positions in this very competitive world. A professional recruiter can offer you many benefits. They are more practiced and skilled at locating passive candidates (those not looking for a job) who might be interested in a new job. They are usually better interviewers. They should also be able to offer advice on how to nail down the detailed standards you want for a specific position; and ideally have the ability to administer and interpret scientific assessment tools.

A professional recruiter will also have a strong background in selecting potential candidates and having effective conversations with them to get at their strengths and weaknesses, resulting in the ability to select a Value-Builder from a crowd of just good or average performers.

Types of Recruiters

There are basically two types of recruiters: retained or contingent. What a retained recruiter does is not the same as what a contingent recruiter does. Their business models differ. A retained recruiter is hired exclusively by a company to locate, assess, and assist in hiring for a specific position the company needs to fill. They are paid as they go so they are fully committed to fill the position. Period. I, as a retained recruiter, have placed several hundred executives and, at least at this point in time, I have never been unsuccessful in completing the assignment (knock wood!).

A contingent recruiter goes out and identifies a wide range of people who might consider or are looking for a new job, and then tries to match those people to jobs being advertised or that they become aware of. A contingent recruiter is more of a clearing-house of resumes, and does not work under an exclusive assignment. His or her fees are contingent on matching a job opening with a candidate in his inventory. Accordingly, a contingent recruiter will throw as many resumes at a client as they can, hoping that one may stick. No offense to my contingent colleagues, but their commitment to the client to fill the position in question is undeniably not as strong as that of a retained recruiter.

Some recruiters say they do both, but I believe that usually means that they don't do either very well. So make sure you understand what type of recruiter you are dealing with.

If you want someone to just be a source of resumes, without offering much value in terms of effectively screening candidates, carefully assessing their professional and personal qualities, and selecting the best options, then a contingent recruiter would work for you. But if you are looking for more services, at a higher level of commitment to ensure you find the right person, then you probably need a retained recruiter. In my experience, companies normally use retained recruiters for key executive positions, which I define as executive roles with a salary of $125K or more for a smaller company. Why?

- A retained recruiter is better equipped to help a company define exactly the needs of the position to be filled.

- A retained recruiter is much more experienced in understanding the roles of executives and spends considerably more time assessing and vetting candidates for their clients.

- Candidates (especially passive candidates) seem more impressed with the commitment of the client and the position to be filled if a retained recruiter is being used.

There is also a significant benefit that retained recruiters provide due to the intensity and effectiveness of their vetting processes. That has to do with the length of the recruiter's guarantee. While a contingent recruiter will usually offer a ninety-day guarantee — that is, if the candidate is fired or quits within 90 days from the start date, the commission paid the recruiter is returned to the client company. But just ninety days? That is simply a poor hire with negative consequences.

A retained recruiter usually offers a one-year replacement guarantee to back up his or her work that the right candidate has been chosen. I go beyond that, offering a two-year replacement guarantee, as I have total confidence in my CompleteFIT executive search process.

If I sound biased, I am. There is a role for both contingent and retained recruiters. But they are not interchangeable.

Getting Status Reports on the Recruitment

No matter what type of recruiter you use, hold their feet to the fire by requesting regular updates and status reports. What have they been doing, how is it going, what are they learning? Every two weeks, I issue a written status report such as that shown on the next page for every executive search that I conduct. It contains key metrics that measure candidate interest levels, where candidates are in the pipeline/process, how many candidates are under active consideration in the queue, and other information that indicates the health of the search assignment. It also contains any key point that I believe the client would find informative.

Status Report 1.1.2018*
COMPANY A — PRESIDENT

EDWARDS EXECUTIVE SEARCH (EES)	
Executive Search Statistics	
#CANDIDATES—PROACTIVE SOURCING	
• Contacted by EES	**244**
• Responded to EES	**132 (54%)**
No Candidate Interest	**98 (74%)**
• Candidates with Interest	**34**
Removed Themselves	**8**
Rejected by EES	**16**
Rejected by Client	**1**
Pending with EES (Q)	**7**
Pending with Client (Q)	**2**
#CANDIDATES—REACTIVE SOURCING	
• Applicants	**753**
• Candidates of Preliminary EES Interest	**53 (7%)**
Removed Themselves	**10**
Rejected by EES	**30**
Rejected by Client	**2**
Pending with EES (Q)	**9**
Pending with Client (Q)	**2**
Candidates Currently Under Consideration = 20 in the Queue (Q)	

*Note how the statistics are segregated by Passive Candidates and Reactive Candidates /Applicants.

STATUS SUMMARY

- The numbers are healthy . . . 997 candidates have been in contact with EES, which is a very positive indicator. 244 passive candidates have been identified and contacted by EES. 753 reactive candidates have applied for the position.

- However, the ratios that measure interest are below the norm.
  - 54% of contacted passive candidates responded to EES vs. a norm of 60%.
  - 74% of those responding had initial interest vs. a norm of 75%.
  - Of the reactive candidates/applicants, 7% were of preliminary EES interest vs. a norm of 10%.

- 87 candidates have been in the EES assessment pipeline.

- Currently, there are 20 candidates under active consideration (in the Queue).

- 4 candidates have been presented to the client by EES with a recommendation for an interview. Their disposition is pending.

- Of the 16 candidates pending with EES, 4 have Hogan results pending and, if there are no issues, will be presented by COB on Thursday.

Thank You for Your Consideration!

I made my first candidate presentation to a client when I was an EVP for a top-five executive search firm, before I started my own firm. Three of us went to see the CEO to present candidates for an SVP Supply Chain position. At the end of the presentation of candidates, the CEO asked us to rank the candidates. So I did. I told him, here's #1 and why, here's #2 and why, and so forth.

As we left the meeting, my colleagues told me never to rank candidates for a client like I had just done, because if the CEO didn't agree, he may not proceed to hire any of them. That was my first inkling that I needed to be on my own. After all, we are being paid a lot of money, and I think the CEO deserved an answer and straightforward, professional advice.

Hiring a Value-Builder is not an academic exercise. It is among the most important decisions any company can make if they are aiming to create a successful leadership team. Hiring the wrong person will have consequences that can take a financial and psychological toll on the firm. Even hiring an OK performer will have an opportunity cost.

The integrity of the CompleteFIT process must be preserved. I am adamant that as a retained recruiter, I am working to find THE best candidate for my clients — a Value-Builder. And, I believe that a Value-Builder needs to be a CompleteFIT. Not just a semi-CompleteFIT. This requires commitment and hard work. It requires the gravitas to offer good advice and well-reasoned recommendations to the client, and as I have said, it requires an effective process.

That is why I take my role as seriously as possible, knowing that my effort to help clients hire a candidate who is truly a CompleteFIT will produce long-term benefits and make their firm's value grow. Placing a Value-Builder into a client company is a very rewarding feeling for me. When my clients' businesses do well, my business does well. I believe that what I have discussed in this book is relevant to all companies. But, to me, it is particularly important to small- to mid-size companies where one executive can make a larger impact.

I wish you every success. I wish you a CompleteFIT. If you need help in finding and hiring one, I can be reached at 312-643-8551.

"Your job description is fairly simple:
Stay in your cubicle and try not to make things worse."

Example of a Confidential Position Specification

I. INTRODUCTION

Our client, Company A is a designer and fabricator of integrated-technology, steel-based products (cabinets, lockers, etc.) sold into a variety of B2B markets.

Located in Atlanta GA, it is an industry leader and global supplier of designed and manufactured turnkey security lockers for several end user markets including amusement parks, athletic and recreational facilities, post offices, etc.

In 2014, Company A decided to expand its product line to include additional metal fabricated products and acquired Company B, a recognized and long standing banner name of quality and precision in the security/storage locker and mailbox industry. Company B sells into a wide array of B2B markets.

The combined entity offers synergistic opportunities in terms of cross selling, new products and operational efficiencies.

Company A is publicly traded on NASDAQ.

For more information, go to . . . www.companyA.com

II. POSITION SCOPE & RESPONSIBILITIES

We are looking for a Sales/Marketing Leader, who has successfully grown the revenues of a business unit into B2B-type markets . . . . **that is significant, not just marginal** revenue growth.

The ideal candidate will have the proven ability to:

- As an individual contributor — identify and close on sales opportunities

- As the chief sales officer — build/reconfigure and lead a sales team; and, improve/reconfigure the Company's selling and sales support processes
- As the chief marketing officer — determine, construct and implement the optimal marketing strategy (product positioning, creation of a value proposition and competitive differentiation, etc.) for the Company's product offerings

This position has sales and management responsibilities for the complete range of Company A's products, both cabinets and customized electronic locker solutions.

We are looking for a Sales/Marketing Leader who can:

1. Identify market and sales opportunities

2. Evaluate revenue and profitability potential; select which opportunities to pursue and set revenue goals

3. Assist in the development of value-added products relevant to the opportunity

4. Develop an effective marketing and selling strategy to successfully penetrate the markets to be served

5. Lead Company A's sales and marketing activities to achieve the revenue goals

III. EXPERIENCE-BASED COMPETENCIES

Industry Relevancy

Primary Industry Experience: Manufacturer of steel-based security cabinets, lockers, containers, etc. sold into B2B markets

Secondary Industry Experience: Manufacturer of any type of security products sold into B2B markets

Tertiary Industry Experience: Manufacturer of fabricated steel-based products sold into B2B markets

Experience-Based Competencies

Required Experience:

- In a sales leadership/management position selling into B2B markets for 10+ years

- In a sales leadership/management position within the Primary, Secondary and/or Tertiary Industry Relevancy definitions above, to YOY double-digit revenue growth

- In direct key account presentation (selling) and the closing of the sale

- In reinvigorating the sales team and selling efforts. From order taker to disciplined business developer

- In building/motivating a highly effective sales team

- In identifying and assessing sales and marketing opportunities:

  ○ Existing products to new customers

  ○ New products to existing customers, utilizing Company A's capabilities

  ○ New products to new customers, utilizing Company A's capabilities.

- In identifying and implementing sales process improvements to facilitate and support significant revenue growth
- A track record of achieving double digit sales growth over a several year period

Preferred Experience:

- In new product development leadership
- In profitability-based customer rationalization and pruning
- In selling through multiple selling channels
- In the electronic marketing and selling of products into B2B markets, via e-commerce platforms, digital marketing, etc.
- In a startup or early phase company
- In building an aftermarket (parts and service) business
- In working with CRM applications
- In selling into government, and other not-for-profit markets

IV. EXECUTIVE SEARCH PROCESS

Company A is committed to hiring the optimal candidate that not only has strong experience-based credentials, but who will fit and thrive in the position of Senior Vice President of Sales & Marketing. As part of the executive search process for this position, candidates will be required to complete an online assessment process to help in that determination.

- The Hogan® Personality Inventory (HPI) and the Hogan® Development Survey (HDS): The HPI evaluates people on seven well-known characteristics that influence occupational success. The HDS measures eleven characteristics that identify performance risks that could impede success.

- The Hogan® Business Reasoning Inventory (HBRI): The HBRI evaluates two types of problem solving; Strategic Reasoning and Tactical Reasoning.

Cultural Competencies (Organization Fit)

Company A believes that a strong cultural alignment is important in an individual's ability to employ all of their skills in a particular environment/culture. As part of the executive search process for this position, finalist candidates will be required to complete an on line assessment to help in that determination.

- The Hogan® Motives, Values, Preferences Inventory (MVPI). The MVPI evaluates individual fit within a corporate culture.

Business Values Competencies (Ethical Fit)

Company A is unequivocally commitment to the highest standards of personal and business ethics and conduct. As part of the executive search process for this position, finalist candidates will be required to write:

1. A concise personal Business Values Credo

2. Responses to two Business Values Scenarios

These exercises are designed to provide information concerning the alignment of business values between client and candidate.

V. EDUCATION REQUIRED/PREFERRED

Required:

- BA/BS in a business, or related, discipline

Preferred:

- Engineering degree, or

- MBA

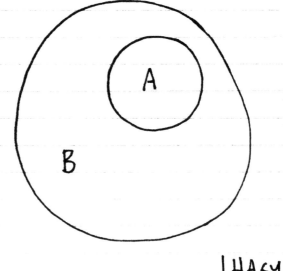

J.HAGY

"A = Your job description
B = What you can do."

Example of a Candidate Experience Matrix —
CONFIDENTIAL — Company A (a pseudonym)

POSITION: VP OF MARKETING

Thank you for your preliminary interest in our client. Your resume indicates that your experience has relevancy to our client's criteria. Accordingly, we may want to speak with you.

In anticipation of our phone conversation, we request that you take some time and evaluate yourself for this position for each of the criteria below. This will make our conversation efficient and focused. It will also help you judge yourself just how strong a fit you are to the position. We will review this information when we speak.

Please feel free to give as much information for your RATIONALE as you care to. We realize this will take some of your time, and we appreciate your consideration. **Thank you.**

We are interested in results, hopefully metric-based results; not opinions, theories, etc.

If you would like to give me information as to your current compensation (Section II) and/or the compensation bandwidth that you would find acceptable before spending your time providing this information, please feel free to do so.

CANDIDATE: _____

BEST NUMBER TO BE REACHED: _____

DATE: _____

SECTION I. QUALIFICATIONS REQUIRED (OR PREFERRED)

Please rate yourself for each criterion, and explain WHY you gave this self-rating i.e. rationale. Please offer facts, examples, and metrics in your explanation.

Ratings: Y1 Very Strong Experience

            Y2 Good Experience

            Y3 Some Experience

             N No Experience

Criteria #1: Relevant Industry Experience —
PRIMARY: Manufacturer of equipment/machinery for the plastic molding industry.

RATING: ⎯⎯⎯⎯⎯⎯⎯⎯⎯⎯⎯⎯⎯⎯⎯⎯⎯⎯⎯⎯⎯⎯⎯⎯

RATIONALE: ⎯⎯⎯⎯⎯⎯⎯⎯⎯⎯⎯⎯⎯⎯⎯⎯⎯⎯⎯⎯⎯

This box will expand as you type. Give Examples & Metrics — Not Your Opinion or Theory

Criteria #2: Relevant Industry Experience —
SECONDARY: Manufacturer of configured and/or custom-engineered industrial equipment/machinery.

RATING: ⎯⎯⎯⎯⎯⎯⎯⎯⎯⎯⎯⎯⎯⎯⎯⎯⎯⎯⎯⎯⎯⎯⎯⎯

RATIONALE: ⎯⎯⎯⎯⎯⎯⎯⎯⎯⎯⎯⎯⎯⎯⎯⎯⎯⎯⎯⎯⎯

This box will expand as you type. Give Examples & Metrics — Not Your Opinion or Theory

Criteria #3: Relevant Industry Experience —
TERTIARY: Manufacturer of mechanical equipment/machinery with electrical controls.

RATING: ⎯⎯⎯⎯⎯⎯⎯⎯⎯⎯⎯⎯⎯⎯⎯⎯⎯⎯⎯⎯⎯⎯⎯⎯

RATIONALE: ⎯⎯⎯⎯⎯⎯⎯⎯⎯⎯⎯⎯⎯⎯⎯⎯⎯⎯⎯⎯⎯

This box will expand as you type. Give Examples & Metrics — Not Your Opinion or Theory

Criteria #4: Relevant Company Experience —
REQUIRED: Marketing Management in a $75MM+ industrial manufacturing company.

RATING: ⎯⎯⎯⎯⎯⎯⎯⎯⎯⎯⎯⎯⎯⎯⎯⎯⎯⎯⎯⎯⎯⎯⎯⎯

RATIONALE: ⎯⎯⎯⎯⎯⎯⎯⎯⎯⎯⎯⎯⎯⎯⎯⎯⎯⎯⎯⎯⎯

This box will expand as you type. Give Examples & Metrics — Not Your Opinion or Theory

Criteria #5: Relevant Job/Position Experience —
REQUIRED: 10+ years industrial Marketing Management.

RATING:

RATIONALE:

This box will expand as you type. Give Examples & Metrics — Not Your Opinion or Theory

Criteria #6: Relevant Job/Position Experience —
REQUIRED: Strategic marketing planning, i.e. product positioning, pricing, competitive strategies, etc.

RATING:

RATIONALE:

This box will expand as you type. Give Examples & Metrics — Not Your Opinion or Theory

Criteria #7: Relevant Job/Position Experience —
REQUIRED: Managing an industrial Product Management function.

RATING:

RATIONALE:

This box will expand as you type. Give Examples & Metrics — Not Your Opinion or Theory

Criteria #8: Relevant Job/Position Experience —
REQUIRED: Driving highly technical product activities —
Product redesign/simplification/rationalization, with the
Engineering department.

RATING: ....

RATIONALE: ....

This box will expand as you type. Give Examples & Metrics — Not Your Opinion or Theory

Criteria #9: Relevant Job/Position Experience —
REQUIRED: In an independent sales rep force environment.

RATING: ....

RATIONALE: ....

This box will expand as you type. Give Examples & Metrics — Not Your Opinion or Theory

Criteria #10: Relevant Job/Position Experience —
REQUIRED: In monitoring competitor activities, to include
pricing, product direction and marketing strategies.

RATING: ....

RATIONALE: ....

This box will expand as you type. Give Examples & Metrics — Not Your Opinion or Theory

Criteria #11: Relevant Company Experience —
PREFERRED: Involvement in the transition from a sales-
driven company culture to a marketing-driven company culture.

RATING: ....

RATIONALE: ....

This box will expand as you type. Give Examples & Metrics — Not Your Opinion or Theory

Criteria #12: Relevant Company Experience —
PREFERRED: Previous experience of Marketing
Management in a larger, state-of-the-art marketing-driven
industrial manufacturing company.

> **RATING:**
>
> **RATIONALE:**

This box will expand as you type. Give Examples & Metrics — Not Your Opinion or Theory

Criteria #13: Relevant Job/Position Experience —
PREFERRED: Managing a tactical Marketing function, i.e.
marketing materials, websites, etc.

> **RATING:**
>
> **RATIONALE:**

This box will expand as you type. Give Examples & Metrics — Not Your Opinion or Theory

Criteria #14: Relevant Job/Position Experience —
PREFERRED: Driving highly technical product activities — New Product Development, with the Engineering
department.

> **RATING:**
>
> **RATIONALE:**

This box will expand as you type. Give Examples & Metrics — Not Your Opinion or Theory

Criteria #15: Relevant Job/Position Experience —
PREFERRED: As a significant contributor in an annual and
long term strategic planning process.

> **RATING:** _____
>
> **RATIONALE:** _____

This box will expand as you type. Give Examples & Metrics — Not Your Opinion or Theory

Criteria #16: Revant Job/Position Experience —
PREFERRED: The effective utilization of a CRM system.

> **RATING:** _____
>
> **RATIONALE:** _____

This box will expand as you type. Give Examples & Metrics — Not Your Opinion or Theory

SECTION II. CASH COMPENSATION HISTORY

	SALARY	BONUS (PAID)	OTHER CASH PAYMENTS
Current Year	$	$	$
Prior Year	$	$	$
Year Before Prior	$	$	$

Current Equity Participation and/or Long-Term Incentives
(if any) & Their Current Value

> **EXPLANATION:** _____
>
> **CURRENT VALUE:** _____

This box will expand as you type. Feel Free to Make Additional Comments

"Could I call you back,
I'm right in the middle of interviews"

Behavioral Interviewing Questions
Used by Edwards Executive Search

I suggest you choose 10 or so of these questions to use during the interview process

ADAPTABILITY

- Describe a major change that occurred in a job that you held. How did you adapt to this change?

- Tell us about a situation in which you had to adjust to changes over which you had no control. How did you handle it?

- Tell us about a time that you had to adapt to a difficult situation.

- What do you do when priorities change quickly? Give one example of when this happened.

AMBITION

- Describe a project or idea that was implemented primarily because of your efforts. What was your role? What was the outcome?

- Describe a time when you made a suggestion to improve the work in your organization.

- Give an example of an important goal that you set in the past. Tell about your success in reaching it.

- Give two examples of things you've done in previous jobs that demonstrate your willingness to work hard.

- How many hours a day do you put into your work? What were your study patterns at school?

- Tell us about a time when you had to go above and beyond the call of duty in order to get a job done.

- Tell us about a time when a job had to be completed and you were able to get it done.

- Tell us about a time when you were particularly effective on prioritizing tasks and completing a project on schedule.

- Tell us about the last time that you undertook a project that demanded a lot of initiative.

- Tell us how you keep your job knowledge current with the on going changes in the industry.

- There are times when we work without close supervision or support to get the job done. Tell us about a time when you found yourself in such a situation and how things turned out.

- What impact did you have in your last job?

- What is the most competitive work situation you have experienced? How did you handle it? What was the result?

- What is the riskiest decision you have made? What was the situation? What happened?

- What kinds of challenges did you face on your last job? Give an example of how you handled them.

- What projects have you started on your own recently? What prompted you to get started?

- What sorts of things have you done to become better qualified for your career?

- What was the best idea that you came up with in your career? How did you apply it?

- When you disagree with your manager, what do you do? Give an example.

- When you have a lot of work to do, how do you get it all done? Give an example?

ANALYTICAL THINKING

- Describe the project or situation which best demonstrates your analytical abilities. What was your role?

- Developing and using a detailed procedure is often very important in a job. Tell about a time when you needed to develop and use a detailed procedure to successfully complete a project.

- Give a specific example of a time when you used good judgment and login in solving a problem.

- Give me a specific example of a time when you used good judgment and logic in solving a problem.

- Give me an example of when you took a risk to achieve a goal. What was the outcome?

- How did you go about making the changes (step by step)? Answer in depth or detail such as "What were you thinking at that point?" or "Tell me more about meeting with that person," or "Lead me through your decision process."

- Relate a specific instance when you found it necessary to be precise in your in order to complete the job.

- Tell us about a job or setting where great precision to detail was required to complete a task. How did you handle that situation?

- Tell us about a time when you had to analyze information and make a recommendation. What kind of thought process did you go through? What was your reasoning behind your decision?

- Tell us about your experience in past jobs that required you to be especially alert to details while doing the task involved.

BUILDING RELATIONSHIPS

- Give a specific example of a time when you had to address an angry customer. What was the problem and what was the outcome? How would you asses your role in diffusing the situation?

- It is very important to build good relationships at work but sometimes it doesn't always work. If you can, tell about a time when you were not able to build a successful relationship with a difficult person.

- Tell us about a time when you built rapport quickly with someone under difficult conditions.

- What, in your opinion, are the key ingredients in guiding and maintaining successful business relationships? Give examples of how you made these work for you.

BUSINESS SYSTEMS THINKING

- Describe how your position contributes to your organization's/unit's goals. What are the unit's goals/mission?

- Tell us about a politically complex work situation in which you worked.

CAUTION

- Have you ever worked in a situation where the rules and guidelines were not clear? Tell me about it. How did you feel about it? How did you react?

- Some people consider themselves to be "big picture people" and others are "detail oriented". Which are you? Give an example of a time when you displayed this.

- Tell us me about a situation when it was important for you to pay attention to details. How did you handle it?

- Tell us me about a time when you demonstrated too much initiative?

COMMUNICATION

- Describe a situation in which you were able to effectively "read" another person and guide your actions by your understanding of their individual needs or values.

- Describe a situation when you were able to strengthen a relationship by communicating effectively. What made your communication effective?

- Describe a situation where you felt you had not communicated well. How did you correct the situation?

- Describe a time when you were able to effectively communicate a difficult or unpleasant idea to a superior.

- Describe the most significant written document, report or presentation which you had to complete.

- Give me an example of a time when you were able to successfully communicate with another person, even when that individual may not have personally liked you, or vice versa.

- Give me an example of a time when you were able to successfully communicate with another person, even when that individual may not have personally liked you.

- Have you ever had to "sell" an idea to your co-workers or group? How did you do it? Did they "buy" it?

- Have you had to "sell" an idea to your co-workers, class-mates or group? How did you do it? Did they "buy" it?

- How do you keep subordinates informed about information that affects their jobs?

- How do you keep your manager informed about what is being done in your work area?

- How do you go about explaining a complex technical problem to a person who does not understand technical jargon? What approach do you take in communicating?

- What kinds of communication situations cause you difficulty? Give an example.

- Tell us about a recent successful experience in making a speech or presentation. How did you prepare? What obstacles did you face? How did you handle them?

- Tell us about a time when you and your current/previous supervisor disagreed but you still found a way to get your point across.

- Tell us about a time when you had to present complex information. How did you ensure that the other person understood?

- Tell us about a time when you had to use your verbal communication skills in order to get a point across that was important to you.

- Tell us about a time when you were particularly effective in a talk you gave or a seminar you taught.

- Tell us about an experience in which you had to speak up in order to be sure that other people knew what you thought or felt.

- Tell us me about a situation when you had to speak up (be assertive) in order to get a point across that was important to you.

- Tell us me about a time in which you had to use your written communication skills in order to get an important point across.

- What challenges have occurred while you were coordinating work with other units, departments, and/or divisions?

- What have you done to improve your verbal communication skills?

- How have you persuaded people through a document you prepared?

- What are the most challenging documents you have done? What kinds of proposals have your written?

- What kinds of writing have you done? How do you prepare written communications?

CONFLICT RESOLUTION

- Describe a time when you took personal accountability for a conflict and initiated contact with the individual(s) involved to explain your actions.

CUSTOMER ORIENTATION

- How do you handle problems with customers? Give an example.

- How do you go about establishing rapport with a customer? What have you done to gain their confidence? Give an example.

- What have you done to improve relations with your customers?

DECISION MAKING

- Discuss an important decision you have made regarding a task or project at work. What factors influenced your decision?

- Everyone has made some poor decisions or has done something that just did not turn out right. Has this happened to you? What happened?

- Give an example of a time in which you had to be relatively quick in coming to a decision.

- Give an example of a time in which you had to keep from speaking or not finish a task because you did not have enough information to come to a good decision. Give an example of a time when there was a decision to be made and procedures were not in place?

- Give an example of a time when you had to be relatively quick in coming to a decision.

- Give me an example of a time when you had to keep from speaking or making a decision because you did not have enough information.

- How did you go about deciding what strategy to employ when dealing with a difficult customer?

- How do you go about developing information to make a decision? Give an example.

- How do you involve your manager and/or others when you make a decision?

- How have you gone about making important decisions?

- How quickly do you make decisions? Give an example.

- In a current job task, what steps do you go through to ensure your decisions are correct/effective?

- Tell us about a time when you had to defend a decision you made even though other important people were opposed to your decision.

- What kind of decisions do you make rapidly? What kind takes more time? Give examples.

- What kinds of problems have you had coordinating technical projects? How did you solve them?

- What was your most difficult decision in the last 6 months? What made it difficult?

- When you have to make a highly technical decision, how do you go about doing it?

DELEGATION

- Do you consider yourself a macro or micro manager? How do you delegate?

- How do you make the decision to delegate work?

- Tell us how you go about delegating work?

- What was the biggest mistake you have had when delegating work? The biggest success?

DETAIL-ORIENTED

- Describe a situation where you had the option to leave the details to others or you could take care of them yourself.

- Do prefer to work with the "big picture" or the "details" of a situation? Give me an example of an experience that illustrates your preference.

- Have the jobs you held in the past required little attention, moderate attention, or a great deal of attention to detail? Give me an example of a situation that illustrates this requirement.

- Tell us about a difficult experience you had in working with details.

- Tell us about a situation where attention to detail was either important or unimportant in accomplishing an assigned task.

EMPLOYEE DEVELOPMENT

- Tell us about a training program that you have developed or enhanced.

EVALUATING ALTERNATIVES

- Have you ever had a situation where you had a number of alternatives to choose from? How did you go about choosing one?

- How did you assemble the information?

- How did you review the information? What process did you follow to reach a conclusion?

- What alternatives did you develop?

- What are some of the major decisions you have made over the past (6, 12, 18) months?

- What kinds of decisions are most difficult for you? Describe one?

- Who made the decision?

FLEXIBILITY

- Have you ever had a subordinate whose performance was consistently marginal? What did you do?

- How have you adjusted your style when it was not meeting the objectives and/or people were not responding correctly?

- What do you do when you are faced with an obstacle to an important project? Give an example.

- When you have difficulty persuading someone to your point of view, what do you do? Give an example.

FOLLOW-UP AND CONTROL

- How did you keep track of delegated assignments?

- How do you evaluate the productivity/effectiveness of your subordinates?

- How do you get data for performance reviews?

- How do you keep track of what your subordinates are doing?

- What administrative paperwork do you have? Is it useful? Why/why not?

INITIATIVE

- Give me an example of when you had to go above and beyond the call of duty in order to get a job done.

- Give me examples of projects/tasks you started on your own.

- Give some instances in which you anticipated problems and were able to influence a new direction.

- How did you get work assignments at your most recent employer?

- What changes did you develop at your most recent employer?

- What kinds of things really get your excited?

- What sorts of projects did you generate that required you to go beyond your job description?

- What sorts of things did you do at school that was beyond expectations?

INTERPERSONAL SKILLS

- Describe a recent unpopular decision you made and what the result was.

- Describe a situation in which you were able to effectively "read" another person and guide your actions by your understanding of their needs and values.

- Tell us about the most difficult or frustrating individual that you've ever had to work with, and how you managed to work with them.

- What have you done in past situations to contribute toward a teamwork environment?

- What have you done in the past to contribute toward a teamwork environment?

INNOVATION

- Can you think of a situation where innovation was required at work? What did you do in this situation?

- Describe a situation when you demonstrated initiative and took action without waiting for direction. What was the outcome?

- Describe a time when you came up with a creative solution/idea/project/report to a problem in your past work.

- Describe something that you have implemented at work. What were the steps used to implement this?

- Describe the most creative work-related project which you have carried out.

- Give me an example of when you took a risk to achieve a goal. What was the outcome?

- Sometimes it is essential that we break out of the routine, standardized way of doing things in order to complete the task. Give an example of when you were able to successfully develop such a new approach.

- Tell us about a problem that you solved in a unique or unusual way. What was the outcome? Were you satisfied with it?

- Tell us about a suggestion you made to improve the way job processes/operations worked. What was the result?

- There are many jobs in which well-established methods are typically followed. Give a specific example of a time when you tried some other method to do the job.

- There are many jobs that require creative or innovative thinking. Give an example of when you had such a job and how you handled it.

- What have been some of your most creative ideas?

- What innovative procedures have you developed? How did you develop them? Who was involved? Where did the ideas come from?

- What new or unusual ideas have you developed on your job? How did you develop them? What was the result? Did you implement them?

- When was the last time that you thought "outside of the box" and how did you do it?

INTEGRITY

- Describe a time when you were asked to keep information confidential.

- Give examples of how you have acted with integrity in your job/work relationship.

- If you can, tell about a time when your trustworthiness was challenged. How did you react/respond?

- On occasion we are confronted by dishonesty in the workplace. Tell about such an occurrence and how you handled it.

- Tell us about a specific time when you had to handle a tough problem which challenged fairness or ethnical issues.

- Trust requires personal accountability. Can you tell about a time when you chose to trust someone? What was the outcome?

INTRODUCING CHANGE

- Have you ever had to introduce a policy change to your work group? How did you do it?

- Have you ever met resistance when implementing a new idea or policy to a work group? How did you deal with it? What happened?

- When is the last time you had to introduce a new idea or procedure to people on this job? How did you do it?

LEADERSHIP

- Give an example of a time in which you felt you were able to build motivation in your co-workers or subordinates at work.

- Give an example of your ability to build motivation in your co-workers, classmates, and even if on a volunteer committee.

- Have you ever had difficulty getting others to accept your ideas? What was your approach? Did it work?

- Have you ever been a member of a group where two of the members did not work well together? What did you do to get them to do so?

- What is the toughest group that you have had to get cooperation from? Describe how you handled it. What was the outcome?

LISTENING

- Give an example of a time when you made a mistake because you did not listen well to what someone had to say.

- How often do you have to rely on information you have gathered from others when talking to them? What kinds of problems have you had? What happened?

- What do you do to show people that you are listing to them?

- When is listening important on your job? When is listening difficult?

MOTIVATING OTHERS

- Have you ever had a subordinate whose work was always marginal? How did you deal with that person? What happened?

- How do you deal with people whose work exceeds your expectations?

- How do you get subordinates to produce at a high level? Give an example.

- How do you get subordinates to work at their peak potential? Give an example.

- How do you manage cross-functional teams?

MOTIVATION

- Describe a situation when you were able to have a positive influence on the actions of others.

- Give an example of a time when you went above and beyond the call of duty.
- Give me an example of a time when you went above and beyond the call of duty.
- How would you define "success" for someone in your chosen career?
- Tell us me about an important goal that you set in the past. Were you successful? Why?

NEGOTIATING

- Describe the most challenging negotiation in which you were involved. What did you do? What were the results for you? What were the results for the other party?
- Have you ever been in a situation where you had to bargain with someone? How did you feel about this? What did you do? Give an example.
- How did you prepare for it?
- How did you present your position?
- How did you resolve it?
- Tell us about the last time you had to negotiate with someone. What was the most difficult part?

ORGANIZATIONAL

- Describe a time when you had to make a difficult choice between your personal and professional life.
- Give me an example of a project that best describes your organizational skills.

- How do you decide what gets top priority when scheduling your time?

- What do you do when your schedule is suddenly interrupted? Give an example.

PERFORMANCE MANAGEMENT

- Give an example of a time when you helped a staff member accept change and make the necessary adjustments to move forward. What were the change/transition skills that you used.

- Give an example of how you have been successful at empowering either a person or a group of people into accomplishing a task.

- How do you handle a subordinate whose work is not up to expectations?

- How do you coach a subordinate to develop a new skill?

- How do you handle performance reviews? Tell me about a difficult one.

- How often do you discuss a subordinate's performance with him/her? Give an example.

- Tell us about a specific development plan that you created and carried out with one or more of your employees. What was the specific situation? What were the components of the development plan? What was the outcome?

- Tell us about a time when you had to take disciplinary action with someone you supervised.

- Tell us about a time when you had to tell a staff member that you were dissatisfied with his or her work.

- Tell us about a time when you had to use your authority to get something done. Where there any negative consequences?

- There are times when people need extra help. Give an example of when you were able to provide that support to a person with whom you worked.

- What have you done to develop the skills of your staff?

- When do you give positive feedback to people? Tell me about the last time you did. Give an example of how you handle the need for constructive criticism with a subordinate or peer.

PERSONAL EFFECTIVENESS

- Give an example of a situation where others were intense but you were able to maintain your composure.

- It is important to maintain a positive attitude at work when you have other things on your mind. Give a specific example of when you were able to do that.

- Keeping others informed of your progress/actions helps them feel comfortable. Tell your methods for keeping your supervisor advised of the status on projects.

- Tell us about a recent job or experience that you would describe as a real learning experience? What did you learn from the job or experience?

- Tell us about a time when you took responsibility for an error and were held personally accountable.

- Tell us about a time when your supervisor criticized your work. How did you respond?

- Tell us about some demanding situations in which you managed to remain calm and composed.

- There are times when we are placed under extreme pressure on the job. Tell about a time when you were under such pressure and how you handled it.

- What have you done to further your own professional development in the past 5 years.

- When you have been made aware of, or have discovered for yourself, a problem in your work performance, what was your course of action? Can you give an example?

PERSUASION

- Describe a situation in which you were able to positively influence the actions of others in a desired direction.

- Describe a situation where you were able to use persuasion to successfully convince someone to see things your way.

- Describe a time when you were able to convince a skeptical or resistant customer to purchase a project or utilize your services.

- Have you ever had to persuade a group to accept a proposal or idea? How did you go about doing it? What was the result?

- Have you ever had to persuade a peer or manager to accept an idea that you knew they would not like? Describe the resistance you met and how you overcame it.

- How do you get a peer or colleague to accept one of your ideas?

- In selling an idea, it is sometimes useful to use metaphors, analogies, or stories to make your point. Give an example of when you were able to successfully do that.

- Tell us about a time when you had to convince someone in authority about your ideas. How did it work out?

- Tell us about a time when you used facts and reason to persuade someone to accept your recommendation.

- Tell us about a time when you used your leadership ability to gain support for what initially had strong opposition.

- Tell us about a time when you were able to successfully influence another person.

PLANNING AND ORGANIZATION

- Describe how you develop a project team's goals and project plan?

- How do you schedule your time? Set priorities? How do you handle doing twenty things at once?

- What do you do when your time schedule or project plan is upset by unforeseen circumstances? Give an example.

- What have you done in order to be effective with your organization and planning?

PRESENTATION

- How do you prepare for a presentation to a group of technical experts in your field?

- How would you describe your presentation style?

- Tell us about the most effective presentation you have made. What was the topic? What made it difficult? How did you handle it?

- What kinds of oral presentations have you made? How did you prepare for them? What challenges did you have?

PROBLEM SOLVING

- Describe the most difficult working relationship you've had with an individual. What specific actions did you take to improve the relationship? What was the outcome?

- Give me an example of a situation where you had difficulties with a team member. What, if anything, did you do to resolve the difficulties?

- Have you ever been caught unaware by a problem or obstacles that you had not foreseen? What happened?

- Tell us about a time when you did something completely different from the plan and/or assignment. Why? What happened?

- What are some of the problems you have faced; such as between business development and project leaders, between one department and another, between you and your peers? How did you recognize that they were there?

- When was the last time something came up in a meeting that was not covered in the plan? What did you do? What were the results of your judgment?

PROBLEM RESOLUTION

- Describe a situation where you had a conflict with another individual, and how you dealt with it. What was the outcome? How do you feel about it?

- Describe a time in which you were faced with problems or stresses which tested your coping skills. What did you do?

- Describe a time when you facilitated a creative solution to a problem between two employees.

- Give a specific example of a time when you used good judgment and logic in solving a problem.

- Give an example of a problem on any job that you have had and tell how you went about solving it.

- Give an example of when you "went to the source" to address a conflict. Do you feel trust levels were improved as a result?

- Problems occur in almost all work relationships. Describe a time when you had to cope with the resentment or hostility of a subordinate or co-worker.

- Some problems require developing a unique approach. Tell about a time when you were able to develop a different problem-solving approach.

- Sometimes the only way to resolve a defense or conflict is through negotiation and compromise. Tell about a time when you were able to resolve a difficult situation by finding some common ground.

- Sometimes we need to remain calm on the outside when we are really upset on the inside. Give an example of a time that this happened to you.

- Tell us about a recent success you had with an especially difficult employee/co-worker.

- Tell us about a situation in which you had to separate the person from the issue when working to resolve issues.

- Tell us about a time when you identified a potential problem and resolved the situation before it became serious.

- There is more than one way to solve a problem. Give an example from your recent work experience that would illustrate this.

PROJECT MANAGEMENT

- Tell us about a time when you influenced the outcome of a project by taking a leadership role.

- Using a specific example of a project, tell how you kept those involved informed of the progress.

RELATE WELL

- Describe a situation where you had to use conflict management skills.

- Describe a situation where you had to use confrontation skills.

- Give me an example of a time when a company policy or action hurt people. What, if anything, did you do to mitigate the negative consequences to people?

- How do you typically deal with conflict? Can you give me an example?

- Tell us about a time when you were forced to make an unpopular decision.

- What would your co-workers (or staff) stay is the most frustrating thing about your communications with them?

REMOVING OBSTACLES

- Have you ever dealt with a situation where communications were poor? Where there was a lack of cooperation? Lack of trust? How did you handle these situations?

- What do you do when a subordinate comes to you with a challenge?

- What have you done to help your subordinates to be more productive?

- What have you done to make sure that your subordinates can be productive? Give an example.

RESOLVING CONFLICT

- Have you ever been in a situation where you had to settle an argument between two friends (or people you knew)? What did you do? What was the result?

- Have you ever had to settle conflict between two people on the job? What was the situation and what did you do?

- Tell us about a time when you had to help two peers settle a dispute. How did you go about identifying the issues? What did you do? What was the result?

RESOURCE MANAGEMENT

- Tell us about a time when you organized or planned an event that was very successful.

SALES

- Describe how you prepare for a sales call for a new client.
- How do you go about making cold calls?
- How have your sales skills improved over the past three years.
- Tell us about your most difficult sales experience.
- Tell us about your sales volume over the past three years. What have you done to influence it?

SCHEDULING

- Describe the most difficult scheduling problem you have faced.
- How did you assign priorities to jobs?
- How did you go about making job assignments?
- When all have been over-loaded, how do your people meet job assignments?

SELF-ASSESSMENT

- Can you recall a time when you were less than pleased with your performance?

- Describe a situation in which you were able to use persuasion to successfully convince someone to see things your way.

- Give me a specific occasion in which you conformed to a policy with which you did not agree.

- Give me an example of an important goal that you had set in the past and your success in reaching it.

- If there were one area you've always wanted to improve upon, what would that be?

- In what ways are you trying to improve yourself?

- Tell us about a time when you had to go above and beyond the call of duty in order to get a job done.

- What do you consider to be your professional strengths? Give me a specific example using this attribute in the workplace.

- What goal have you set for yourself that you have successfully achieved?

- What was the most useful criticism you ever received?

SELECTING AND DEVELOPING PEOPLE

- How do you coach an employee in completing a new assignment?

- What have you done to develop your subordinates? Give an example.

- What have you done to improve the skills of your subordinates?

- What was your biggest mistake in hiring someone? What happened? How did you deal with the situation?

- What was your biggest success in hiring someone? What did you do?

SETTING GOALS

- Did you have a strategic plan? How was it developed? How did you communicate it to the rest of your staff?

- How do you communicate goals to subordinates? Give an example.

- How do you involve people in developing your unit's goals? Give an example.

- What company plans have you developed? Which ones have you reached? How did you reach them? Which have you missed? Why did you miss them?

- What goals did you miss? Why did you miss them?

- What goals have you met? How did you do to meet them?

- What were your annual goals at your most current employer? How did you develop these goals?

- What were your long-range plans at your most recent employer? What was our role in developing them?

SETTING PERFORMANCE STANDARDS

- How do you go about setting goals with subordinates? How do you involve them in this process?

- How do you let subordinates know what you expect of them?

- What performance standards do you have for your unit? How have you communicated them to your subordinates?

SETTING PRIORITIES

- Have you ever been overloaded with work? How do you keep track of work so that it gets done on time?

- How do you manage your time?

- How do you schedule your time?

- When given an important assignment, how do you approach it?

SOUND JUDGMENT

- Describe a situation when you had to exercise a significant amount of self-control.

- Give me an example of a time in which you had to be relatively quick in coming to a decision.

- Give me an example of when you were able to meet the personal and professional demands in your life yet still maintained a healthy balance.

- Give me an example of when you were responsible for an error or mistake. What was the outcome? What, if anything, would you do differently?

- If you were interviewing for this position what would you be looking for in the applicants?

- We work with a great deal of confidential information. Describe how you would have handled sensitive information in a past work experience. What strategies would you utilize to maintain confidentiality when pressured by others?

• When have you had to produce results without sufficient guidelines? Give an example.

STRATEGIC PLANNING

• Describe what steps/methods you have used to define/ identify a vision for your unit/position.

• How do you see your job relating to the overall goals of the organization?

• In your current or former position, what were your long and short-term goals?

• Tell us about a time when you anticipated the future and made changes to current responsibilities/operations to meet future needs.

STRESS MANAGEMENT

• How did you react when faced with constant time pressure? Give an example.

• People react differently when job demands are constantly changing; how do you react?

• What kind of events cause you stress on the job?

• What was the most stressful situation you have faced? How did you deal with it?

TEAMWORK

• Describe a situation in which you had to arrive at a compromise or help others to compromise. What was your role? What steps did you take? What was the end result?

- Describe a team experience you found disappointing. What would you have done to prevent this?

- Describe a team experience you found rewarding.

- Describe the types of teams you've been involved with. What were your roles?

- Describe your leadership style and give an example of a situation when you successfully led a group.

- Give an example of how you have been successful at empowering a group of people in accomplishing a task.

- Give an example of how you worked effectively with people to accomplish an important result.

- Have you ever been a project leader? Give examples of problems you experienced and how you reacted.

- Have you ever been in a position where you had to lead a group of peers? How did you handle it?

- Have you ever participated in a task group? What was your role? How did you contribute?

- Please give your best example of working cooperatively as a team member to accomplish an important goal. What was the goal or objective? To what extent did you interact with others on this project?

- Some people work best as part of a group—others prefer the role of individual contributor. How would you describe yourself? Give an example of a situation where you felt you were most effective.

- Tell us about a time that you had to work on a team that did not get along. What happened? What role did you take? What was the result?

- Tell us about a work experience where you had to work closely with others. How did it go? How did you overcome any difficulties?

- Tell us about the most difficult challenge you faced in trying to work cooperatively with someone who did not share the same ideas? What was your role in achieving the work objective?

- Tell us about the most difficult situation you have had when leading a team. What happened and what did you do? Was it successful? Emphasize the "single" most important thing you did?

- Tell us about the most effective contribution you have made as part of a task group or special project team.

- Think about the times you have been a team leader. What could you have done to be more effective?

- What is the difficult part of being a member, not leader, of a team? How did you handle this?

- What role have you typically played as a member of a team? How did you interact with other members?

- When is the last time you had a disagreement with a peer? How did you resolve the situation?

- When working on a team project have you ever had an experience where there was strong disagreement among team members? What did you do?

TIME MANAGEMENT SCHEDULE

- Describe a situation that required you to do a number of things at the same time. How did you handle it? What was the result?

- How do you determine priorities in scheduling your time? Give an example.

- How do you typically plan your day to manage your time effectively?

- Of your current assignments, which do you consider to have required the greatest amount of effort with regard to planning/organization? How have you accomplished this assignment? How would you asses your effectiveness?

TOUGHNESS

- Managers have to make tough decisions. What was the most difficult one you have had to make?

- Tell us about setbacks you have faced. How did you deal with them?

- What has been your major work related disappointment? What happened and what did you do?

- What is the most competitive situation you have experienced? How did you handle it? What was the result?

- What was your major disappointment?

VARIETY

- How many projects do you work on at once?
- When was the last time you made a key decision on the spur of the moment? What was the reason and result?
- When was the last time you were in a crises? What was the situation? How did you react?
- Which of your jobs had the most rapid change? How did you feel about it?

VALUES DIVERSITY

- Give a specific example of how you have helped create an environment where differences are valued, encouraged and supported.
- Tell us about a time that you successfully adapted to a culturally different environment.
- Tell us about a time when you had to adapt to a wide variety of people by accepting/understanding their perspective.
- Tell us about a time when you made an intentional effort to get to know someone from another culture.
- What have you done to further your knowledge/understanding about diversity? How have you demonstrated your learning?
- What have you done to support diversity in your unit?
- What measures have you taken to make someone feel comfortable in an environment that was obviously uncomfortable with his or her presence?

Acknowledgments

I would like to thank Debby Edwards and
Anna Edwards Haynam for their unconditional love,
support and encouragement.

I would also like to thank my editor Rick Benzel
for his assistance in editing and organizing this book
and Susan Shankin for her cover and page design work.
Their professionalism is to be commended.

About the Author

MR. EDWARDS is a diversified business leader. He has run companies, started companies, bought companies, integrated companies and sold companies. He has served as a Director or Trustee for numerous civic and business organizations.

Mr. Edwards graduated from Colgate University. He attended Harvard University's Executive Leadership Program as a Danforth Fellow.

After receiving his MBA from Washington University's Olin Graduate School of Business, Mr. Edwards spent the first fifteen years of his career managing consumer product business units for major corporations such as General Mills, Pillsbury and INTERCO.

In 1989, he and a group of partners acquired The Ansehl Company from Weyerhaeuser Corporation. Ansehl was a leading manufacturer/marketer of private-label health and beauty care products sold through mass merchandisers, chain drug stores, and supermarkets. Mr. Edwards served as President/

CEO of Ansehl until December 2000 when he sold the company to a strategic buyer.

Since the sale of Ansehl, Mr. Edwards has focused his professional activities on the sourcing and optimization of human capital. In 2002, he joined a top-five executive search firm as an Executive Vice President. Believing that there was a better approach to executive search, in 2004 he started his own retained executive search firm, Edwards Executive Search, continuing to serve a national client base in placing C-level and other key executives. He currently serves as Managing Partner of Edwards Executive Search (www. edwards-search.com) and has successfully placed CEOs, CFOs, General Counsels, VPs of Sales/Marketing, Operations, Finance, Engineering, Manufacturing, Supply Chain, and Crisis Managers, among others.

Mr. Edwards' business background is unique for an executive recruiter. As a former CEO and multi-company Director, he understands, and has experienced firsthand, the value of effective talent acquisition, or conversely the cost and disruption of executive underperformance and turnover due to a less-than-optimal executive hire. He believes that the effectiveness of talent acquisition can be significantly improved with a thorough, systematic, and professional hiring process. He has been trained and designated as a Master Career Coach and is certified in the application and interpretation of several leading scientific selection and development assessment tools. He has earned Black Belts in both Lean/Six Sigma and Tae Kwon Do.

82520622R00113

Made in the USA
Lexington, KY
03 March 2018